PACEM IN TERRIS:
ITS CONTINUING RELEVANCE FOR
THE TWENTY-FIRST CENTURY

*Papers from a Symposium Held at the United Nations
in New York City on 24 October 2012 in Preparation for
the 50th Anniversary of the Famous 1963 Encyclical Letter of
Blessed Pope John XXIII on World Peace*

FRANCIS DUBOIS & JOSEF KLEE
Editors

*Pacem in Terris Press Series
Postmodern Catholic Social Teaching*

PACEM IN TERRIS PRESS
http://paceminterris.net

This book is published with gratitude to
Sr. Claudia Carlin and Pierian Press for earlier permission to use
papal quotations from Sr. Carlin's multivolume edited collection
THE PAPAL ENCYCLICALS.

ISBN-13: 978-1489571182
ISBN-10: 1489571183

PACEM IN TERRIS PRESS

is the publishing service of the
Pacem in Terris Global Leadership Ecumenical Initiative
which is sponsored by

PAX ROMANA
CATHOLIC MOVEMENT FOR INTELLECTUAL & CULTURAL AFFAIRS
USA

1025 Connecticut Avenue NW, Suite 1000
Washington DC 20036
http:paceminterris.net

With special gratitude to
the generous donors who made the Symposium possible:

SOVEREIGN MILITARY ORDER OF MALTA

EQUESTRIAN ORDER OF THE HOLY SEPULCHRE OF JERUSALEM

MS. MARIA ALMEIDA

MS. ASTRID HORAN

MS. UDA KLEE

And also to the volunteer organizers for the event:

MS. MARIA ALMEIDA

MS. ALEJANDRA C. ROSERO

TABLE OF CONTENTS

PREFACE

Pacem in Terris Press Series
on Postmodern Catholic Social Teaching[1]

JOE HOLLAND, PH.D.

President, Pax Romana /Catholic Movement for Intellectual & Cultural Affairs - USA

Professor of Philosophy & Religion, St. Thomas University, Miami Gardens, Florida

T his is the second book in the Pacem in Terris Press Series on Postmodern Catholic Social Teaching. As President of Pax Romana / Catholic Movement for Intellectual and Cultural Affairs – USA, which is the sponsor of Pacem in Terris Press, I offer my personal gratitude, and the gratitude of our directors and members, to everyone who made possible this important volume.

Postmodern Catholic Social Teaching was founded by Blessed Pope John XXIII, whose papacy ran from 1958 to 1963. So it may be called the "Johannine" stage of Catholic Social Teaching, after its prophetic founder.

---

[1] Copyright © 2013 Joe Holland.

This new stage of the tradition follows the earlier stage known as "Modern Catholic Social Teaching." It was founded by Pope Leo XIII, whose papacy ran from 1878 to 1903. So it may be called the Leonine stage, after its prophetic founder. The Leonine stage, or Modern Catholic Social Teaching, was largely focused on the Western industrial countries during the second stage of the Industrial Revolution, which grew out of the Machine Revolution of the second half of the 19th century.[2]

The Machine Revolution was made feasible by new refinements in steel, and eventually also by electrification and the rise of petro-chemical industries. In turn, it made feasible mass industrial production, which broke beyond the earlier limits of "manufacture" (from its Latin roots, meaning "made by hand"). Mass production was then accompanied by mass consumption and also by mass social movements, including the modern labor movement, as well as by development of the modern industrial state.

Following the Russian Revolution of 1917, this second stage of the Industrial Revolution saw the earlier industrial countries, which had followed the modern ideology of Liberal Capitalism, challenged by the rise of the first industrial country proclaiming the alternative modern ideology of Scientific Socialism, namely Soviet Russia. The conflict between these two ideological systems then led to the 20th century's Cold War, and eventually within it to the apocalyptic doctrine of "Mutually Assured Destruction" (MAD).

---

[2] For more on the Leonine stage of Catholic Social Teaching, and also on the earlier pre-Leonine stage, see my book MODERN CATHOLIC SOCIAL TEACHING: THE POPES CONFRONT THE INDUSTRIAL AGE 1740-1958 (Paulist Press, 2004).

Blessed John XXIII's great 1963 encyclical letter PACEM IN TERRIS (Peace on Earth), which this volume addresses, was issued by John at the height of the Cold War, indeed at its climax, in order to propose a post-ideological vision of peace for the global human future.

The core strategy of the Leonine stage of Modern Catholic Social Teaching had been to resist Scientific Socialism and to reform Liberal Capitalism, and to create a new form of Christian Civilization grounded in a social and philosophical reform of the liberal-capitalist ideology.

Leo had sought social reform by supporting workers' unions and by promoting a regulatory and social-welfare revision of the modern laissez-faire liberal state. He had also sought philosophical reform by countering the atomistic-mechanical philosophy undergirding Liberal Capitalism with a revival of the communitarian-organic philosophy of Thomas Aquinas, which was rooted in the philosophy of Aristotle (rejected by leading Western intellectuals at the birth of the modern Western era).

During the middle years of the 20th century the social reforms of Liberal Capitalism, supported early on by Leo, finally succeeded for many workers and their families in Western industrialized nations. This took the form of social democracy in Western Europe and the "New Deal" in the United States, with similar reforms in other industrialized liberal-capitalist countries.

But philosophical reform proved more difficult, and eventually impossible. For both liberal and Marxian philosophers largely continued to support ever more deeply the reductionist mate-

3

rialism of the atomistic-mechanical philosophy at the foundation of the modern Western cultural project.[3]

In addition, during the second half of the 20th century multiple new global challenges arose on the horizon. These included:

- Liberation, but also continued impoverishment, of the countries formerly colonized by Western imperialism;

- Parallel racial-ethnic struggles within industrialized countries and their former colonies;

- Systemic violation of human rights by dictatorial-totalitarian states of both the left (communism) and the right (fascism);

- Rising emancipation of women, who had suffered under millennia of misogyny and patriarchy;

- Clear and present danger of global thermonuclear destruction;

- Realization that both modern reductionist and materialist ideologies were leading the human family, and all of life in the Earth Community, on a slow but steady path of unsustainable ecological devastation;

These new global challenges led to the end of the Leonine strategy of Modern Catholic Social Teaching, and to the birth of the new Johannine strategy of Postmodern Catholic Social Teach-

---

[3] For more on this philosophical dimension of the modern Western cultural project, and across both modern materialist ideologies, see my essay at the end of this volume.

ing. There are significant differences between the two strategies.

- Whereas the Leonine strategy of Catholic Social Teaching
  had largely addressed the Western industrialized nations
  of Liberal Capitalism, the Johannine stage now addresses
  the entire human family in all nations across the globe.

- Whereas the Leonine strategy had rejected Scientific Socialism and tried both socially and philosophically to reform
  Liberal Capitalism, the Johannine strategy proclaims the
  philosophical bankruptcy of both modern materialist ideologies. In doing so, it also seeks to serve the birth of a new
  global civilization which will be humanistic and ecological,
  as well as spiritual, yet not formally a "Christian Civilization."

- Whereas the Leonine strategy had prohibited Catholics
  from dialoguing or cooperating with socialists, the Johannine strategy calls for dialogue and cooperation with all
  people of good will, including socialists. In so doing, the
  Johannine strategy distinguishes between philosophical errors which it rejects and human persons of good will, who
  may hold those errors but with whom it seeks to dialogue
  and cooperate. It seeks such dialogue and cooperation in
  order to help create a new global civilization which will
  transcend the philosophical errors of both dominant modern industrial ideologies – again, Liberal Capitalism and
  Scientific Socialism.

Further, the Johannine strategy retrieves an important theme
originally present in Leo's vision but often forgotten in its later

expressions. This is the argument that "development" should not displace human communities in the rural agricultural sector, but should enhance them. This piece of both the Leonine and Johannine strategies may be described as an implicit commitment to what today is called "agroecology."[4] Thus, while the initial pursuit of the Johannine vision carried as its global slogan "justice and peace," its full unfolding needs to be understood as embracing "justice, peace, and ecology."

In addition, one more challenge has arisen for Postmodern Catholic Social Teaching – not in the area of social ethics but rather in the area of bioethics, though this challenge has also become a social one. This additional challenge is the late modern technological attack on the dignity of human life, initially from mass abortion, later from euthanasia, and more recently from dangerous tendencies in genetic engineering like "posthumanism" and "transhumanism" (due to misguiding of modern science by its underlying atomistic-mechanistic cosmology). All together this attack on the dignity of human life may prove a prelude a larger attack on that principle from an emerging revival of eugenics.

Sadly, however, many contemporary Catholics across the globe have become antagonistically polarized between the often "left-leaning" pursuit of social ethics and the often "right-leaning" pursuit of bioethics. Healing that tragic split remains a major task for the still developing Johannine stage of Catholic Social Teaching. But to address that problematic further we would

---

4 See *http://www.agroecology.org* (accessed 2013-05-15).

need yet another book, which hopefully Pacem in Terris Press can explore in the future.

In sum, the new Johannine stage of Postmodern Catholic Social Teaching is calling us to seek a fresh global civilization, which will go beyond both modern industrial ideologies, which will support a regenerative vision of life embracing justice, peace, and ecology, and which will integrate social ethics and bioethics.

Just as in the past Leo XIII's famous 1891 encyclical RERUM NOVARUM stood out as the "Magna Charta" of the Modern Catholic Social Teaching, so Blessed John XXIII's famous 1963 encyclical PACEM IN TERRIS stands out today as the "Magna Charta" of Postmodern Catholic Social Teaching.

Hopefully, this small and humble volume constitutes an important effort to help us to understand and to implement John's prophetic vision for a renewal of the entire human family and of the entire Earth Community, including a renewal of the global Catholic tradition, the wider global Christian tradition, and all the spiritual traditions of the human family.

2

INTRODUCTION

Pacem in Terris, the United Nations, and Pax Romana

AMBASSADOR FRANCIS DUBOIS

JOSEF KLEE, PH.D.

Co-Directors, Pax Romana CMICA-USA New York Office
for the United Nations

O n 24 October 2012 at United Nations Headquarters in New York City, the Permanent Observer Mission of the Holy See and the Sovereign Military Order of Malta, in cooperation with our project "Pax Romana at the United Nations," convened the Symposium titled "The Encyclical Pacem in Terris: Its 50th Anniversary and Its Relevance to the 21st Century." The event was held in preparation for that anniversary in 2013.

Pacem in Terris Encyclical

The papal encyclical PACEM IN TERRIS was issued by Blessed Pope John XXIII on 11 April 1963. It was John's final encyclical, as he died from cancer two months after its completion. In this document, for the first time in a papal encyclical, John included among those to whom it was addressed *all people of good will.*

In this work, his "peace encyclical," John responded to the global political situation in the middle of the Cold War. The document was issued two years after the erection of the Berlin Wall and only a few months after the Cuban Missile Crisis. In it, John explained that conflicts *should not be resolved by recourse to arms, but rather by negotiation.*

He further emphasized the importance of respect for human rights, and he declared *that everyone has the right to life, to bodily integrity, and to the means which are suitable for the proper development of life.*

The encyclical is divided into four sections.

- The first section establishes the order among human beings, encompassing human rights and moral duties.

- The second section addresses the relationship between humans and state, dwelling on the collective authority of the latter and its responsibility for the common good.

- The third section establishes the need for order and equality among nations, and the need for states to be subject to rights and duties that the individual must also abide by, and with special attention to the problem of atomic weapons.

- The fourth section presents the relationship between nations and the world community, thus resulting in collective states assisting other states, with special praise for the role of the United Nations Organization (UN) and its Universal Declaration of Human Rights.

The encyclical ends by urging Catholics to be active in public life for the common good of the human family, to seek a synthesis of scientific-technological achievements and spiritual values, and to cooperate in these tasks with other Christians and all reasonable persons of moral integrity.

Finally, the conclusion distinguishes between error and persons in error. While rejecting error, it urges dialogue and collaboration with persons in error for the sake of the world peace as called for by the Prince of Peace.

PACEM IN TERRIS paved the way for strong involvement of Catholic faith-based organizations in the promotion of human rights, justice, and peace-building through peaceful resolution of conflicts.

United Nations

The encyclical PACEM IN TERRIS praises the work of the United Nations, which each year celebrates its birthday on 24 October – the same day on which this Symposium was convened.

The UN is the world's largest, foremost, and most prominent international organization. It was founded in 1945 after World War II to replace the League of Nations, to stop wars between countries, and to provide a platform for dialogue. Its stated aims include promoting and facilitating cooperation in international law, international security, economic development, social progress, human rights, civil rights, civil liberties, political freedoms, democracy, and the achievement of lasting world peace.

For these purposes, the United Nations contains multiple subsidiary organizations to carry out its missions. Since 2011, the United Nations has had 193 member states.

Pax Romana at the UN

Pax Romana is one of the oldest international lay Catholic movements. It was created in two stages with two branches:

- First, in 1921, as a lay movement of Catholic university students

- Second, in 1947, as a lay movement of Catholic intellectuals and professionals

The first branch is called in English the "International Movement of Catholic Students" (IMCS), and the second branch is called in English the "International Catholic Movement for Intellectual and Cultural Affairs" (ICMICA). Both branches work together to serve the need to build a peaceful and just world.

Pax Romana, the name which both branches share in common, referred originally to the peace for which its leaders worked in cooperation with the papacy after World War I. The name was given to the movement in 1921 by Pope Benedict XV, when he reportedly said to its leaders: *you are my Pax Romana*.

Pax Romana, as both movements working in partnership, has the highest level consultative status with the Economic and Social Council of the United Nations. It maintains NGO (non-governmental organizational) representatives at UN offices in New York, Paris, Geneva, Vienna, and Nairobi. It is also a member of CONGO (Committee of NGOs having official relationship with the United Nations). In addition, for the Canon Law of the Catholic Church, Pax Romana is recognized as a private organization and it is accredited to the Pontifical Council for the Laity of the Holy See ("Vatican").

To assist the work of Pax Romana at the United Nations in New York, Pax Romana / Catholic Movement for Intellectual and Cultural Affairs - USA (CMICA), a US federation of ICMICA, sponsors its New York Office for the United Nations. "Pax Romana at the United Nations" is the core project of this New York Office. The project offers its services to assist the work of IMCS and ICMICA representatives on the Pax Romana NGO team at the United Nations in New York.

Pax Romana CMICA-USA also sponsors a UN-oriented and semester-long internship for law students from St. Thomas University School of Law in Miami Gardens, Florida. This program is directed by Dr. Mark Wolff, Professor of Law at St. Thomas University School of Law. Also, Dr. Wolff is currently the Main Representative of Pax Romana at the United Nations in New York. Students in this law-internship program are assigned legal work in United Nations offices, in offices of member-state missions at the United Nations, and in offices of intergovernmental and nongovernmental organizations accredited to the UN.

Further, our "Pax Romana at the UN" project sponsors in New York City an ongoing seminar for UN-related individuals interested in Catholic Social Teaching. This seminar meets one evening per month for prayer, study, and dialogue.

In conclusion, we are pleased that the 2012 Symposium at the United Nations in New York, "The Encyclical Pacem in Terris: Its

50th Anniversary and Its Relevance to the 21st Century," turned out so well. We are equally pleased that this book of papers from the Symposium is being published. And we thank the many people who made possible the event and the book.

For more information about the work of
"Pax Romana at the UN"
please contact:

PAX ROMANA CMICA-USA
NEW YORK OFFICE FOR THE UNITED NATIONS

1011 First Avenue, Seventh Floor
New York NY 10022
Phone: +1 (646) 794-2268
Email: pax.romana@archny.org

OPENING REMARKS

The Encyclical, the Holy See,
and the Order of Malta at the United Nations

AMBASSADOR ROBERT L. SHAFER

Permanent Observer of the Sovereign Military Order of Malta
to the United Nations

G reetings, Your Excellency Archbishop Francis A. Chullikatt, professors, officials, experts, and confreres. This is a
remarkable gathering in commemoration of a revolutionary document, the encyclical PACEM IN TERRIS, which was issued by Pope
John XXIII on April 11, 1963.

This was the first encyclical addressed to *all people of good will*, the
broadest possible audience, as opposed to earlier encyclicals
which were directed to church leaders. It is an optimistic document in which Pope John XXIII gives a vision of a moral order that
should prevail among humans, among persons and states, among
states, and within the world community. As such, it relates natu-
rally to the mission of the United Nations.

Pope John XXIII emphasized the importance of respect for human
rights, which flows from the Christian understanding that *every*

person has the right to life, to bodily integrity, and to the means which are suitable for the proper development of life.

The legacy of PACEM IN TERRIS is unmistakable. Its influence is seen in the ongoing work of the Holy See Mission here at the United Nations. Its influence is also seen in the work that is done here and worldwide by the Sovereign Military Order of Malta, which I am privileged to represent here at the United Nations.

Founded in the 11th century in Palestine, the Order of St. John of Jerusalem of Rhodes and of Malta is one of the oldest institutions of Western and Christian Civilization, Our lay religious order is uniquely dedicated to serving the sick and the poor – based on the teaching of the Gospels and echoing the Christian ideals expressed so timelessly in PACEM IN TERRIS.

The work of the Order also dovetails with the goals of the Church in its outreach to the socially isolated, the victims of persecution, and refugees of any race and religious faith. Our 13,500 Knights and Dames of our Order worldwide have recently provided assistance and aid to Haiti after tropical storm Isaac, as well as to Syrian refugees in Lebanon, and they have built 35 new health care centers in South Sudan.

We join in solidarity with the Holy See Mission as we look to PACEM IN TERRIS, the "peace encyclical," for an ongoing blueprint and inspiration for our work towards the nobler vision of public life that honors the dignity of each human person as a child of God.

REFLECTIONS BY THE PAPAL NUNCIO

The Encyclical's Historical Background and Contemporary Relevance

MOST REVEREND FRANCIS A. CHULLIKATT, J.C.D.
Titular Archbishop of Ostra, Apostolic Nuncio, and
Permanent Observer of the Holy See to the United Nations

E xcellencies, distinguished guests, ladies and gentleman. It is a great pleasure to welcome you all this afternoon. In particular, I would like to thank Dr. Joseph Klee and Ambassador Francis Dubois, both of Pax Romana, for organizing this event, as well as Ambassador Robert Shafer for co-sponsoring it. Finally, I would like to welcome our distinguished panelists; your insights and contribution here today are an important means for further analysing and understanding the impact of the Encyclical PACEM IN TERRIS.

Today, as we gather to study and reflect on the teaching and contribution of this landmark papal document to the Church's Social Doctrine, we are reminded that the mark left by this encyclical goes far beyond the social teaching of the Church and has touched a generation of policy makers and people around the world. It had a great impact on the world fifty years ago, and it still has much to contribute to peace, justice, freedom, charity, and truth in the present age!

Historical Background of Pacem in Terris

At the peak of the Cold War, when the world was divided and driven by fear of the menace of a nuclear war, when the destructive idea of "Mutually Assured Destruction" (MAD) created an uneasy and deadly *détente*, and only a few short months after the Cuban missile crisis and two years after the erection of the Berlin Wall, Pope John XXIII took this time of great division to exercise his pastoral mission and vision to write an "open letter to the world." For it was addressed not only to members of the Church, other Christians, and other believers; it was also directed specifically to *all people of good will* everywhere. This must not be ignored or forgotten.

In fact, it would take people of good will to address the human manufactured problems that threatened humanity's existence then as today. Now, fifty years later, his message is as timely today as it was then, and it is a letter which still serves as a reminder of the work we must all do in order to build international peace and understanding not only for the short term but for the rest of human history.

In drafting the papal encyclical, Pope John XXIII sought to build upon the teachings of his predecessors whose reigns coincided with the two world wars, and to respond not only to international juridical developments following the conclusion of these wars, but also to speak to the particular exigencies of his times.

While some of these exigencies have been dispelled temporarily, their seeds are still with us; moreover, new concerns, such as terrorism and regional or global rivalries, threaten us in the present age.

However, in any case, we must recall that John XXIII was not only shaped by the times in which he lived and labored for God's people, but he was also shaped by his formation and training as a diplomat—someone who seeks not glory but just resolutions to conflict that will endure.

In addition, Pope John XXIII's confident hopefulness in PACEM IN TERRIS towards the post-war international juridical order owed much to the Second Vatican Council, convened by him only the previous year.

The openness of the Church to the modern world and its desire to respond to the signs of the times are reflected in PACEM IN TERRIS, particularly in considering science and technology as catalysts for bringing together peoples and nations in relationships of economic, cultural, and social dimensions referred to in the encyclical as *social progress*.[1]

The novelty of Blessed John XXIII's approach in PACEM IN TERRIS, then, is that the Pope was able in the circumstances of the times to bring to bear his own rich experiences in international affairs by pronouncing for the first time in papal teaching on the development of an international juridical reality based on the time-tested moral reasoning of the Natural Law, and expressly to name in this

---

[1] PACEM IN TERRIS, n. 88.

regard the recent establishment of the United Nations Organization.

While Pope John did not align the international juridical order which he described in PACEM IN TERRIS specifically with the United Nations, nevertheless, his explicit naming of it represented a great encouragement to the then fledgling organization.

His vision of a new juridical order did not go unnoticed. Shortly after the release of the encyclical, the United Nations Secretary-General, U Thant, recognized in the principles of PACEM IN TERRIS a juridical order in harmony with the purposes and objectives of the United Nations.[2] And Adlai Stevenson, the US Ambassador to the United Nations at the time, remarked that in this historic encyclical Pope John had left the world an inspiring charter for the future of mankind.

In addition, PACEM IN TERRIS was declared by the Council of Europe to be one of the "great charters" of history. Moreover, within days of Pope John's death in 1963 and a few months removed from his own, President John Kennedy declared to the world that, as a Catholic, he was proud of the encyclical. But Kennedy did not stop there, for he further asserted that, as an American, he could learn from it.

PACEM IN TERRIS also represents the first time a papal encyclical addressed the fundamental importance of the Universal Declaration of Human Rights. PACEM IN TERRIS describes the 1948 Declara-

---

[2] UNITED NATIONS REVIEW 10 (June 1962) 33.

tion as an *important step on the path towards the juridical-political organization of all the peoples of the world.*[3]

What Pope Leo XIII's 1891 Encyclical, RERUM NOVARUM, had done for advancement in the economic and social fields, PACEM IN TERRIS was considered to offer for the improvement of the international order.

The NEW YORK TIMES remarked that the Pope's identification of commonalities binding together all peoples as a fundamental aspect of human nature could serve as a bridge spanning divisions over doctrinal, racial or other matters.[4] After all, bridge-building is implicit in the title of any pope as *pontifex maximus!*

In addition, Pope John's evaluation of the United Nations is nuanced. Only if it succeeds, through its structures and methods, to be worthy of the nobility of its tasks, can the United Nations be relied upon effectively to safeguard the dignity of all members of the human family.[5]

The safeguarding of every member of the human family was just as crucial in 1963 as it is fifty years later. Yet, many in the world then, as today, must be reminded of this fact that is crucial to the survival of the human race, and John XXIII understood this well.

---

[3] PACEM IN TERRIS, n. 143-144.

[4] NEW YORK TIMES, April 14 1963, Section IV, 8.

[5] PACEM IN TERRIS, n. 145.

Pacem in Terris' Relevance for Today

Today we might wonder what this encyclical, PACEM IN TERRIS, still has to offer to a society that has gone through significant political turmoil and transformation since 1963.

However, when we read the encyclical, we immediately realize that even after half-a-century the vision and the practical wisdom offered by Pope John XXIII still have much to teach us in our continued and relentless struggle to face the new challenges for peace and justice in the post-Cold War era, especially amid the continued proliferation of armaments, in particular, weapons of mass destruction.

Moreover, the wisdom of John XXIII presented in this extraordinary letter also tells us much about who we are and what is the nature of the human person that is defined not by the state but by our Creator. But his wisdom also equips us to address in a responsible and just fashion the threat of terrorism that engulfs the present age.

Today, we still confront many of the challenges indentified by John XIII. In particular, we continue to witness the powerful nations working to modernize their nuclear arsenal and continuing to use nuclear weapons as a key deterrent, a ploy to perpetuate the illicit retention of these deadly and destructive weapons, a portent of an apocalyptic annihilation of humanity from the face of the Earth.

In the area of disarmament and non-proliferation, for example, the international community for too long has been unable to come together to address the unresolved problem of 20,000 nuclear weapons around the world. For almost fifteen years we have witnessed the continued growth of military spending which only begins to slow in the face of a global financial crisis. In addition, we have seen the number of states with nuclear capability increase, and there seems to be no end in sight to this senseless, unnecessary, and dangerous multiplication. In this regard, it is significant what the encyclical writes:

> *The world will never be the dwelling-place of peace, till peace has found a home in the heart of each and every human person, till all preserve within themselves the order ordained by God to be preserved.*[6]

As we know, at the heart of the Church's social doctrine is the anthropology which recognizes in each of us the image and likeness of our Creator, endowed with intelligence and freedom, capable of knowing, understanding, and loving, and which bestows on us that transcendental human dignity. As a result,

> *... peace and justice are fruits of the right order that is inscribed within creation itself, written on human hearts[7] and accessible to all people of good will, all pilgrims of truth and of peace.*[8]

We know this because, as the words of Blessed John XXIII remind us, the Creator instilled in each person the gift of reason to comprehend the intelligible reality that surrounds us, whereby we acknowledge the essential need for the natural moral law.

---

[6] PACEM IN TERRIS, n.165.

[7] ROMANS 2:15.

[8] Message of Pope Benedict XVI to the Pontifical Academy of Social Sciences, 27 April 2012.

The encyclical, PACEM IN TERRIS, stands as a powerful summons, resonating the call of the Second Vatican Council, to commit ourselves and to engage in that creative dialogue and interaction between the Church and the world, between believers and non-believers, and between peoples and cultures.

Why? Well, as Blessed John reminds us, we must comprehend the fact that everyone is a person created in the image of God and endowed with both fundamental natural rights and corresponding duties. The Church, therefore, shaping herself thoroughly on the Christian vision of every human being's destiny in the world, wants to proclaim a message of reconciliation, peace, and hope to a humanity that is hungry for it, a message that could be welcomed and embraced by people of all beliefs or none at all.

It was in light of that same spirit, in the aftermath of the deplorable terrorist attacks of September 2001, that Blessed John Paul II reaffirmed his message to the world: that there can be *no peace without justice, no justice without forgiveness*.[9] These words of vital significance were built on the keen intellect and broad shoulders of John XXIII.

The notion of forgiveness, dear friends, needs to be highlighted in international debate on conflict resolution. It can transform the sterile and confrontational language of mutual recrimination and revenge which benefits no one and leads nowhere. If human beings are made in the image and likeness of God, a God of justice

---

[9] Message for the World Day of Peace, 2002.

who is *rich in mercy*,[10] then such qualities need to be re-proposed and reintroduced in the conduct of human affairs.

As Pope Benedict XVI reminded us, it is the combination of justice and forgiveness, of justice and grace, which lies at the heart of the divine response to human wrong-doing[11] – at the heart, in other words, of the *divinely established order*.[12]

Forgiveness is not a denial of wrong-doing, but a participation in the healing and transforming love of God which reconciles and restores.[13] Forgiveness and reconciliation form the key that opens the door for a better future for everyone; revenge, by contrast, precludes this promise from materializing.

We have learned from the past that historic wrongs, abuses, and injustices can only be overcome if men and women are inspired by a message of healing, pardon, and hope, a message that offers a way forward, out of the deadlock that so often locks, fetters, and imprisons peoples and nations into a vicious circle of violence, revenge and retribution.

Since 1963, some of the conflicts that seemed insoluble at the time have now been consigned to history, because those involved acknowledged to themselves and one another the durable justice that can be achieved when reconciliation, rather than revenge, becomes the objective.

---

[10] EPHESIANS 2:4.

[11] SPES SALVI, n. 44.

[12] PACEM IN TERRIS, n. 1.

[13] Message of Pope Benedict XVI to the Pontifical Academy of Social Sciences, 27 April 2012.

When facing bitter and painful moments of injustice, violence, and war, protesting against God in the name of justice is not helpful because a world without God will always be a world without hope.[14] Only God can create authentic justice as He is the way, the truth, and the life.[15] And faith gives us the certainty that he does so. God is justice and creates justice.[16] This is our consolation and our hope.

In this world, scourged and scarred by various struggles and conflicts, twisted and warped by lies and vanity, this is the message of hope, justice, and peace which PACEM IN TERRIS wants to re-propose to today's society and to the international community. God has shown us the goal and has also given us the tools to seek it. We have been given the intelligence to understand this, and we have been given the freedom and desire to follow the path that will take us there.

Let us take heart, then, as we struggle for peace and justice in the world today, Let us be confident that our common pursuit of the divinely established order – of a world where the dignity of every human person is upheld and accorded the respect that is due – can dispel the darkness of war, violence and discord, and fill it with the light of peace, harmony and hope. Thank you for the attention.

---

[14] Cf. *Eph* 2:12.

[15] Jn 14:6.

[16] Cf. Encyclical Letter of Pope Benedict XVI, SPES SALVI, n.44.

5

PACEM IN TERRIS & DISARMAMENT

The Encyclical's Continuing Relevance for Global Stability and Security

PIERCE S. CORDEN, PH.D.

Visiting Scholar, Center for Science, Technology and Security Policy,
American Association for the Advancement of Science

T hanks to Josef Klee and to Pax Romana for inviting me to make a few remarks this afternoon about PACEM IN TERRIS and its relevance to disarmament – to moving away from reliance on war as a basis for international security. It is an honor to be here. My remarks are in a personal capacity.

United Nations Charter

The following objectives laid out in the Preamble of the UNITED NATION CHARTER,

> ... to save succeeding generations from the scourge of war ... to
> ensure, by the acceptance of principles and the institution of

methods, that armed force shall not be used, save in the common interest,[1]

are made operational by the Charter's obligations regarding the use of peaceful means to adjudicate disputes, and regarding aggression and self-defense. An international system for global security and stability in which the use of force is increasingly diminished is consistent with these provisions. The United Nations today pursues the realization of that system.

Disarmament

The term disarmament is at times considered idealistic. Other terms are used. Arms-control is one. Non-proliferation and its variants, such as counter-proliferation, are others. The use of force means the use of weapons, but disarmament means eliminating weapons. Other terms relate to this objective but can support both the process and the end of peace. So, while using the term disarmament, we can bear in mind the wide range of agreements and undertakings that it embraces.

Cuban Missile Crisis

We are during this week also observing the fiftieth anniversary of another seminal event of our age, the Cuban Missile Crisis. PACEM IN TERRIS is recognized as a response to that nerve-wracking brush with global catastrophe. It sought to address head-on the nuclear arms race between the United States and the Soviet Union, a race supported by an extravagance of atmospheric nuclear-weapon tests, and the exposure of everyone in the world to the radioactivi-

---

[1] *http://www.un.org/en/documents/charter/preamble.shtml*

ty which those tests released into the environment. Arms-racing is the exact opposite of disarmament.

PACEM IN TERRIS eloquently addressed the perilous situation of that time – speaking in paragraph 111 of a conflagration set off *by some unexpected and unpremeditated act* and, while recognizing that *the monstrous power of modern weapons acts as a deterrent*, stating that

> *... there is nevertheless reason to fear that the mere continuance of nuclear tests, undertaken with war in mind, can seriously jeopardize various kinds of life on Earth.*

Limited Agreements for Disarmament

PACEM IN TERRIS was issued on Holy Thursday, April 11, 1963. On that day only one agreement addressing nuclear weapons was in force: the Antarctic Treaty, which prohibits on that continent the installation and testing of not only nuclear but all weapons, and provides for inspections to verify compliance.

Today, a panoply of international undertakings has been negotiated to constrain nuclear and other weapons: the Limited Test Ban Treaty, signed later in 1963; the vital Nuclear Non-Proliferation Treaty of 1968; the series of bilateral US-USSR, and now Russian, strategic arms limitation and reduction agreements; the conventions outlawing biological and chemical weapons; constraints on conventional weapons in Europe; and many others.

But these agreements – important as they are in placing bricks in the disarmament wall against the use of military force in interstate conflict – have not yet resulted in a process for confidently reversing the massive buildup in strategic weapons, to reach levels approaching zero. And since 1963 the number of states that are acknowledged nuclear-weapon powers has increased from three to eight, with ominous signs that even further proliferation may occur. Already in 1960, John F. Kennedy had voiced his deep concern that nuclear proliferation ranked as a most serious threat to international peace and security.

Thus, it cannot be said that achievements in disarmament to date have launched the world on a secure trajectory toward the objective – shared almost universally by the international community – of nuclear disarmament and *a treaty on general and complete disarmament under strict and effective international control,* as Article VI of the Non-Proliferation Treaty would have it.

Continuing Relevance of Pacem in Terris

What might we therefore say about the relevance of PACEM IN TERRIS now, as we contemplate the objective of disarmament, seemingly in the distant future?

- As we deal with disputes in Europe over ballistic-missile defense, and see no movement on conventional weapons and sub-strategic nuclear weapons?

- As we note the years-long impasse in the Conference on Disarmament to negotiation of a ban on the production of fissile material for nuclear weapons?

- As we consider the worsening conflict in Syria (and its acknowledged possession of chemical weapons), the confrontations in the Middle East, the unsettled situation in South Asia and in the Pacific, and the violent conflicts in Africa?

- As we contend with the great burden of military expenditures?

In paragraph 98, PACEM IN TERRIS treats of mutual relations among nations, which *must be regulated by the norm of truth and justice.* But, in recognizing that civil authority exists to protect *above all else the common good of that particular civil society,* it goes on to say that this common good *certainly cannot be divorced from the common good of the entire human family.* Paragraph 99 continues this thought, saying that civil societies

> ... *must join their plans and forces whenever the efforts of an individual government cannot achieve its desired goals; but in the execution of such common efforts, great care must be taken lest what helps some nations should injure others.*

In paragraph 113 Pope John XXIII says

> ... *the fundamental principle on which our present peace depends must be replaced by another, which declares that the true and solid peace of nations consists not in quality of arms but in mutual trust alone.*

And he voices his confidence that it can be achieved. However far in the future, a peaceful international order, that will consist of mutual trust alone, can be a matter for contemplation. But the recognition (in paragraph 137) that the international order – the universal common good – requires more than free-wheeling states is crucial; it points toward the shared sovereignty embodied in disarmament agreements. Already in paragraph 112 PACEM IN TERRIS teaches

> *... that the stockpiles which exist in various countries should be reduced equally and simultaneously by the parties concerned; that nuclear weapons should be banned, and finally that all come to an agreement on a fitting program of disarmament, employing mutual and effective controls.*

These teachings about the global common good remain entirely relevant for the ongoing efforts of the United Nations in its First Committee. They are equally relevant for the efforts of the Conference on Disarmament in Geneva; of the international organizations dealing with atomic energy, chemical weapons and nuclear testing; of the bilateral nuclear arms reduction forum (which will of necessity become multilateral); and of many other forums – all efforts to wrestle to submission the hydra-headed weapons creature.

The language may differ – arms control or non-proliferation for disarmament, and verification of compliance for mutual and effective controls – but the essential meaning is the same.

We hardly need to be reminded of the urgency of pursuing the enterprise of disarmament. What is the alternative? Today's armed conflicts, and conflicts risking wider war, even the use of nuclear weapons? This is at best a metastable state, not one of global stability and security.

Thus PACEM IN TERRIS provides an enduring basis for the work of disarmament.

Conclusion

I want to conclude by making a few observations about deterrence. We are this year also commemorating the fiftieth anniversary of the convening of the Second Vatican Council, which promulgated its pastoral constitution, GAUDIUM ET SPES, on December 7, 1965. Its paragraph 81 links to disarmament the call in PACEM IN TERRIS for a public and universal authority. It acknowledges that

> ... *the defensive strength of any nation is considered to be dependent upon its capacity for immediate retaliation ... (and that) an accumulation of arms ... serves, in a way heretofore unknown, as deterrent to possible enemy attack.*

But GAUDIUM ET SPES rejects this as *a safe way to preserve a steady peace* and urges us to *make use of the interlude granted us from above* to discover a better way.

The United States Catholic Bishops pastoral letter, THE CHALLENGE OF PEACE: GOD'S PROMISE AND OUR RESPONSE, will have its thirtieth anniversary in 2013. The bishops' letter also takes account of the provisional role of nuclear deterrence.

I think we should ask the question whether this conditional and temporary acceptance of deterrence has perhaps inadvertently dulled the impetus to establish a global security architecture that all three documents call for.

How long is temporary? More decades? The 22nd century?

Did the conclusions of these documents – that a sort of interim ethic of deterrence might be justified – envision accepting without strong protest the halting and limited progress to date?

Is all energy and effort being concentrated on eliminating what remains the most perilous threat to humanity?

The tolerance of deterrence on an interim basis by the Church, as by governments, perhaps constitutes a certain prudence. And prudence is a virtue. But the Church has, in its teaching responsibility, a prophetic role.

PACEM IN TERRIS can be understood as a prophetic document, a teaching aimed at energizing not only Catholics, but persons of all faith persuasions, or none at all, to work with great determination to make the world different.

I think that, as we skate on the edge of the abyss, the prophetic is also the prudent. Thus, the Church at all levels might prudently take up afresh the teachings in PACEM IN TERRIS, and bring its moral influence to bear on all governments to make the work of disarmament the preeminent task. Weapons enterprises seem quite capable of taking care of themselves.

6

PACEM IN TERRIS & HUMAN RIGHTS

The Encyclical's Teaching that

Peace Is Possible Only with the Fullness of Human Rights

ELIZABETH F. DEFEIS, J.D., LL.M.[1]

Professor of Law & former Dean

Seton Hall University School of Law

W hen PACEM IN TERRIS was issued in 1963, AMERICA, the Jesuit weekly, wrote:

Ultimately, the Encyclical's true greatness may be seen to consist in this, that it gave voice in our day to all humankind's authentic aspiration for lasting peace in a world order based on justice, truth, charity and freedom.[2]

Still Relevant Today

The relevance of PACEM IN TERRIS to human rights can best be understood when viewed from a historical perspective. The parallels

---

[1] The author wishes to thank Sarah Jafari, Research Assistant, Seton Hall University School of Law, Class of 2013, Maja Basiolo, Associate Professor and Research Librarian, and Mary Malfitano, Legal Support Specialist.

[2] AMERICA, 604, April 27, 1963.

that exist with the events of today then become readily apparent. The Encyclical calls attention to certain characteristics or "signs of the times" which had become increasingly apparent in the world of the sixties.

Let me cite just a few. Pope John XXIII notes that:

- Nations are achieving their independence[3]

- Workers are claiming their rights in the socio-economic sphere[4]

- Women are becoming ever more conscious of their human dignity[5]

More and more nations are forming governments and devising constitutions that include a charter of fundamental human rights or a bill of rights.[6]

The very conditions which Pope John XXIII drew attention to fifty years ago are significant today. In the 1960s nations were emerging from repressive regimes as colonial empires crumbled. These new regimes were struggling to find a voice in the world community. New systems of governance that would respect human rights and dignity both nationally and internationally were being discussed and in a few cases achieved.

---

[3] PACEM IN TERRIS (Encyclical of Pope John XXIII on Establishing Universal Peace in Truth, Justice, Charity, and Liberty) Par. 42, April 11, 1963.

[4] *Supra* note 2, at par. 40.

[5] *Supra* note 2, at par. 41.

[6] *Supra* note 2, at par. 75.

The protection of human rights had moved to the forefront of the newly created international organization—the United Nations.[7] Both the Civil Rights movement and the movement for Women's Rights were effecting changes in society, not only in the United States, but also throughout the world

How do these events resonate today? Only recently, long entrenched dictators have been overthrown and new governments are starting to emerge.[8] New constitutions are being drafted, and there are persistent calls for human rights to be respected and included.[9] As the global economic crises continue, workers are resisting the reduction of benefits that they had previously ob-

---

[7] U.N. CHARTER, art. 1, par. 3. The UN Charter in its Preamble states:

We the peoples of the United Nations determined to save succeeding generations from the scourge of war, which twice in our lifetime has brought untold sorrow to mankind, and to reaffirm faith in fundamental human rights, in the dignity and worth of the human person, in the equal rights of men and women and of nations large and small, and to establish conditions under which justice and respect for the obligations arising from treaties and other sources of international law can be maintained, and to promote social progress and better standards of life in larger freedom …

[8] Angelique Chrisafis and Ian Black, *Zine al-Abidine Ben Ali Forced to Flee Tunisia as Protesters Claim Victory*, THE GUARDIAN (Jan. 14, 2011), *http://www.guardian.co.uk/world/2011/jan/14/tunisian-president-flees-country-protests*; Leila Fadel, *With Peace, Egyptians Overthrow a Dictator*, THE WASHINGTON POST, (Feb. 11, 2011), *http://www.washingtonpost.com/wp-dyn/content/article/2011/02/11/AR2011021105709.html.*

[9] Human Rights Watch, *Egypt: Fix Draft Constitution to Protect Key Rights*, (Oct. 8, 2012), *http://www.hrw.org/news/2012/10/08/egypt-fix-draft-constitution-protect-key-rights*; Sharif Adbel Kouddous, *Will Egypt's New Constitution Take the Country Backwards?*, THE NATION (Oct. 9, 2012), *http://www.thenation.com/article/170447/will-egypts-new-constitution-take-country-backwards#.*

tained.[10] The brutality and oppression that particularly affect women are now recognized as a violation of basic human rights.

At the same time, our world today has become even more fragmented and plagued by religious and ethnic strife.[11] Human rights and dignity are under attack as never before, but there is also hope. New generations are aspiring for a world order based on the principles outlined in PACEM IN TERRIS, namely, justice, truth, and charity and, as Pope John XXIII emphasized, by freedom as well.

In PACEM IN TERRIS, Pope John XXIII made human rights the centerpiece of his Encyclical devoted to peace. A central message is that peace is possible only if and when the rights of every human being are addressed.[12]

These human rights are universal, inviolable, and inalienable.[13] Further, every human being is endowed with these rights by virtue of her or his personhood as an aspect of a person's dignity.[14]

---

[10] Kristen Spillane, *Rioters Push for Change amid Spanish Economic Hardships*, THE MIAMI HURRICANE (Oct. 18, 2012),
http://www.themiamihurricane.com/2012/10/18/rioters-push-for-change-amid-spanish-economic-hardships/; Raphael Minder, *Backlash Grows against Austerity Plan in Portugal*, THE NEW YORK TIMES (Oct. 15, 2012),
http://www.nytimes.com/2012/10/15/world/europe/backlash-grows-against-austerity-plan-in-portugal.html?pagewanted=all.

[11] The Pew Forum on Religion & Public Life, RISING TIDE OF RESTRICTIONS ON RELIGION, (Sept. 2012),
http://www.pewforum.org/uploadedFiles/Topics/Issues/Government/RisingTideofRestrictions-fullreport.pdf.

[12] *Supra* note 2, at par 165.

[13] *Supra* note 2, at par 145.

[14] *Supra* note 2, at par 9.

What are these basic human rights? In 1948, the United Nations General Assembly adopted the UNIVERSAL DECLARATION OF HUMAN RIGHTS without dissent.[15] It was the first human rights instrument that was open to all nations for adoption. In PACEM IN TERRIS, Pope John characterized the UNIVERSAL DECLARATION OF HUMAN RIGHTS as an act of the highest importance, while Pope John Paul II called it *the joy for all people of good will*.[16]

Full Range of Human Rights

The rights outlined in the UNIVERSAL DECLARATION OF HUMAN RIGHTS include not only civil and political rights but also economic, social and cultural rights. In the United States, civil and political rights such as freedom of speech, religious liberty, and due process of law are stressed, while social rights such as the right to food, shelter, education, and health care are neglected or ignored. This conception of rights is much narrower than the concept of rights protected by international law.

Pope John XXIII embraced the international view by discussing human rights in terms of economic, social and cultural rights, as well as by stressing civil and political rights. The list of human rights outlined in the Encyclical are all encompassing. Some of the rights that Blessed John names, in the order in which they are listed, include:

---

[15] *See* United Nations General Assembly, UNIVERSAL DECLARATION OF HUMAN RIGHTS, 10 December 1948. *http://www.un.org/en/documents/udhr*.

[16] Pope John Paul II, REDEMPTOR HOMINIS, Encyclical letter on the Redeemer of Man (St Paul Edition. 1979).

- The right to life, bodily integrity, food, clothing, shelter, rest, medical care, necessary, social services

- The right to respect for one's person, good reputation, freedom to search for truth, freedom of speech

- The right to share in the benefits of culture and education, freedom of worship

- Freedom to choose one's state in life and to form a family

- Freedom of initiative in the economic field

- The right to work

- The right to adequate working conditions, proper wage, private property, even of productive goods

- Freedom of assembly and association

- Freedom of movement and residence

- The right to emigrate and immigrate

- The right to active participation in public affairs

- The right to juridical protection of rights and right to act freely and responsibly[17]

Human rights are sometimes divided into three so-called generations of rights.

- The first generation lists the civil and political rights, such as speech and religious liberty.

- The second generation lists the economic and social rights, such as rights to health care, shelter, and education.

---

[17] *Supra* note 2, at pars. 11-29 for all of the above enumerated rights.

- The third generation lists collective rights, such as peace and development.

Pope John XXIII sets out the basic principles that are at the core of the human rights system. The first is the paramount importance of human dignity[18] – unfortunately, a concept that we in the United States are less than familiar with when discussing human rights.

Some consider human dignity too vague or indefinite to be enforced, but it is prominently mentioned in the UNIVERSAL DECLARATION OF HUMAN RIGHTS and in the international human rights conventions.[19] The recently adopted CHARTER OF FUNDAMENTAL RIGHTS FOR THE EUROPEAN UNION devotes its first chapter to "Human Dignity."[20]

Some national constitutions emphasize human dignity. For example, human dignity is the fundamental principle of the German Constitution. The first article reads: *Human Dignity shall be inviolable. To respect and protect it shall be the duty of all state authority.*[21]

---

[18] *See supra* note 2, at pars. 35, 38, 41, 48, 112, 122.

[19] United Nations General Assembly., UNIVERSAL DECLARATION OF HUMAN RIGHTS, art. 23.

[20] European Union, CHARTER OF FUNDAMENTAL RIGHTS OF THE EUROPEAN UNION, art, 1. 7, December 2000, OFFICIAL JOURNAL OF THE EUROPEAN COMMUNITIES, 18 December 2000 (2000/C 364/01).

[21] GRUNDGESETZ [GERMANY CONSTITUTION], May 23, 1949, art. I, sect. 1; For a discussion of "Dignity" as an expressive norm, *See* Tarunabh Khaitan, *Dignity as an Expressive Norm: Neither Vacuous Nor a Panacea*, 32, OXFORD JOURNAL OF LEGAL STUDIES 1 (2012).

Framework for Human rights

PACEM IN TERRIS outlines the framework for the system of human rights.

- First, PACEM IN TERRIS emphasizes that each human being is endowed with intelligence and free will, and possesses, as an aspect of human dignity, rights and duties which are universal, inviolable, and inalienable.[22]

- Second, just as the encyclical affirms human rights, so it argues that duties must also be respected. Each right obligates others to acknowledge and respect those rights. Each right carries with it a corresponding duty. For example, there is a social duty in the right of private property.

- Third, the goal of the social order and civil authorities is the attainment of the Common Good. As Pope John points out, *The attainment of the common good is the sole reason for the existence of civil authorities.*[23]

- Finally, every human right derives its moral force from Natural Law.[24] And laws that are contrary to the moral order and to the will of God are not binding on the conscience of citizens.

How are these principles applied and how do they address some of the pressing human rights problems that we are facing today—

---

[22] *Supra* note 2, at par. 48.

[23] *Supra* note 2, at par. 54.

[24] *Supra* note 2, at par. 30, "*Every basic human right draws its authoritative force from the natural law, which confers it and attaches to it its respective duty.*"

such as the situation of refugees, threats to religious liberty, and oppression based on race or sex?

Plight of Refugees

The plight of refugees today is one of the most pressing problems facing the international community. At the time that PACEM IN TERRIS was written, persons were fleeing totalitarian regimes. The Berlin Wall had been erected, and on this continent many from Cuba were seeking asylum in the United States.[25]

Today, 67 million people have been forced to flee their homes due to conflict or natural disaster. Sixteen million are refugees and 51 million are internally displaced persons.[26] As of this writing, there are more than a quarter of a million refugees from Syria alone, with the greatest numbers fleeing to Turkey and Jordan.[27]

Pope John XXIII recognized the suffering endured by refugees, and called upon members of the international community to address the situation. His words, uttered in 1963, could not be more relevant today. He said:

> *Our heart makes it impossible for us to view without bitter anguish of spirit the plight of those who for political reasons have*

---

[25] Joyce A. Hughes, *Flight from Cuba*, 36 CALIFORNIA WESTERN LAW REVIEW, 39, 40 (1999).

[26] The Global Refugee Crisis, AMERICAN REFUGEE COMMITTEE (Nov. 19, 2012), *http://www.arcrelief.org/site/PageServer?pagename=learn_globalrefugeecrisis.*

[27] Nick Cumming-Bruce and Neil MacFarquhar, *Relief Crisis Grows as Refugees Stream Out of Syria*, THE NEW YORK TIMES (Nov. 19, 2012), *http://www.nytimes.com/2012/09/12/world/middleeast/relief-crisis-grows-as-refugees-stream-out-of-syria.html.*

been exiled from their own homelands. There are great numbers of such refugees at the present time, and many are the sufferings – the incredible sufferings – to which they are constantly exposed.[28]

Refugees are persons and all their rights as persons must be recognized.

Refugees cannot lose these rights simply because they are deprived of citizenship of their own States … Among one's personal rights we must include his right to enter a country in which one hopes to be able to provide more fittingly for oneself and one's dependents. It is therefore the duty of State officials to accept such immigrants and—so far as the good of their own community, rightly understood, permits—to further the aims of those who may wish to become members of a new society.[29]

Pope John then singled out for praise those persons and international agencies working to alleviate the plight of such refugees.[30] He seemed to be speaking directly to governments and persons throughout the world today on issues relating to asylum, citizenship, and humanitarian relief.

Religious Liberty

Religious Freedom is a basic human right that all persons possess by virtue of their humanity. It enjoys a special status among the

---

[28] *Supra* note 2, at par. 103.

[29] *Supra* note 2, at ¶ 105-106.

[30] *Supra* note 2, at ¶ 107-108.

fundamental rights and freedoms rooted in the dignity of the person.[31]

PACEM IN TERRIS affirms the right of human beings *to worship God in accordance with the right dictates of one's own conscience, and to profess one's religion both in private and in public*[32] This right is based on the obligation to serve God rightly and on the Church's right to liberty.[33] And yet, today, religious liberty is under attack as never before.

On his visit to Lebanon in 2012, Pope Benedict XVI addressed the theme of religious freedom or religious liberty. On that occasion he stated:

> *Religious freedom is the basic right on which many other rights depend. The freedom to profess and practice one's religion without danger to life and liberty must be possible to everyone ... Religious freedom has a social and political dimension which is indispensible for peace ... It does not impose itself by violence but rather by force of its own truth.*[34]

Intolerance, discrimination, and violence suffered by religious minorities not only continue, but also appear to be escalating. A

---

[31] Pope Benedict XVI, WORLD DAY OF PEACE MESSAGE, par. 5, January 1, 2011.

[32] *Supra* note 2, at par. 14.

[33] John Langan, *Human Rights in Roman Catholicism*, in Charles E. Curran & Richard A. MacCormick, MORAL NORMS AND CATHOLIC TRADITION: READINGS IN MORAL THEOLOGY, VOL.1 (Paulist Press, 1979), 14.

[34] Address of His Holiness Pope Benedict XVI, Apostolic Journey to Lebanon on Sep. 145, 2012 (Nov. 19, 2012), *http://www.vatican.va/holy_father/benedict_xvi/speeches/2012/september/documents/hf_ben-xvi_spe_20120915_autorita_en.html.*

report issued in September 2012 by the Pew Forum on Religion and Public Life estimated that 75% of the world's population lives in countries with high government restrictions or high social hostilities involving religion.[35] This is up from 70% a year ago.[36] Government actions that were measured include an outright ban on some religions, preaching, or conversions.[37] Actions of private individuals or groups measured include mob violence and harassment.[38] The report further indicates that Christians are most at risk, and are the subject of such intolerance in more than 110 countries.[39]

Such actions of states, or acquiescence by states, are of course a violation of international law. International treaties and declarations of United Nations bodies provide the norms and standards against which actions of governments and individuals should be measured. Article 18 of the UNIVERSAL DECLARATION OF HUMAN RIGHTS provides in part that:

> *Everyone has the right to freedom of thought, conscience and religion … and freedom, either alone or in community with others and in public or private, to manifest his religion or belief in teaching, practice, worship and observance.*[40]

This right is far-reaching and profound. The Human Rights Committee of the United Nations has stated that *"it encompasses freedom*

---

[35] *Supra* note 10, at 9.

[36] *Id.*

[37] *Id.* at 11.

[38] *Id.*

[39] *Id.* at 24.

[40] *Supra* note 18, at art. 18.

of thought on all matters, personal conviction and the commitment to religion or belief, whether manifested individually or in community with others."[41] The terms belief and religion are construed broadly and protect atheistic beliefs as well as newly established or religious minorities.[42]

Religious freedom is considered so fundamental in international law that, unlike other human rights guarantees such as speech rights, it cannot be derogated from, even in times of public emergency.[43]

PACEM IN TERRIS initiated the dialogue on religious liberty within the Church, which was further developed in The DECLARATION ON RELIGIOUS LIBERTY of Vatican II. The document

> *... declares that the human person has a right to religious freedom. This freedom means that all persons are to be immune from coercion on the part of individuals or of social groups and of any human power, in such wise that no one is to be forced to act in a manner contrary to one's own beliefs ... The Council further declares that the right to religious freedom has its foundation in the very dignity of the human person as this dignity is known through the revealed word of God and by reason itself. This right of the human person to religious freedom is to be rec-*

---

[41] Human Rights Committee, General Comment 22, Art. 18 (Forty-eighth session, 1993). Compilation of General Comments and General Recommendations Adopted by Human Rights Treaty Bodies, U.N. Doc. HRI/GEN/1/Rev.1 at 35 (1994).

[42] *Id.*

[43] Human Rights Committee, General Comment 29, States of Emergency (article 4),
U.N. Doc. CCPR/C/21/Rev.1/Add.11 (2001).

ognized in the constitutional law whereby society is governed and thus it is to become a civil right.[44]

Pope Benedict XVI stressed the importance of interfaith dialogue. He stated:

A pluralistic society can only exist on the basis of mutual respect, the desire to know the other and continuous dialogue ... It cannot be forgotten that religious freedom is the basic right on which many other rights depend. The freedom to profess and practice one's religion without danger to life and liberty must be possible to everyone.[45]

What can we conclude? Although sufficient international legal instruments exist that affirm and protect religious liberty, as with many of the human rights guarantees, implementation is lacking.

Discrimination on the basis of religion violates principals of equality and non-discrimination, which form the basis of the international human rights regime. PACEM IN TERRIS was issued at a time when religion was under attack by some totalitarian governments.

---

[44] Pope Paul VI , Declaration On Religious Freedom *Dignitatis Humanae* - On The Right Of The Person And Of Communities to Social And Civil Freedom in Matters Religious Promulgated by His Holiness, (December 7, 1965); Angela Carmella, John Courtney Murray, S.J., THE TEACHINGS OF MODERN CHRISTIANITY ON LAW, POLITICS AND HUMAN NATURE, Vol. I. 115 (John Witte Jr. and Frank Alexander, eds. Columbia University Press, 2006); Vatican Radio, *Vatican: We Stand for Religious Liberty*, Sept. 13, 2012,
http://en.radiovaticana.va/news/2012/09/13/vatican:_we_stand_for_religious_liberty/e n1-620645.

[45] Edward Pentin, *Pope Benedict XVI's Visit to Lebanon-Full Texts*, NATIONAL CATHOLIC REGISTER (Nov. 20, 2012), *http://www.ncregister.com/blog/edward-pentin/pope-benedict-xvis-visit-to-lebanon-full-texts; See also supra note 2.*

Fifty years later, religious liberty is once again threatened, albeit from a different source.

As we confront intolerance and violence today, it is well to remember the teachings of PACEM IN TERRIS:

> *Among one's rights is that of being able to worship God in accordance with the right dictates of one's own conscience, and to profess one's religion both in private and in public.*[46]

Protection of religious liberty is clearly the challenge of the Human Rights Community today. All segments of the International Community including states, international organizations, civil society and faith-based groups have a role to play, if this challenge is to be successfully met.

Equality of Women

Blessed John XXIII affirmed the equality of all human beings by reason of their natural dignity. Thus neither sex nor race nor economic class can form the basis for denying or restricting the rights of human persons.

Let us focus for a moment on the situation of women. A half century ago, the role of women was undergoing dramatic changes. New legislation prohibiting discrimination on the basis of sex in areas such as employment was being enacted. Women were entering the workforce in increasing numbers. Pope John explicitly noted the increasing participation of women in public life, which impelled them to claim *the rights and duties which belong to them as*

---

[46] *Supra* note 2, at 14.

human persons.[47] And yet 50 years have passed, and women continue to face oppression and discrimination, which appear to be increasing.

Nicholas Kristof, one of the preeminent commentators of today, noted that in the 19th Century the paramount moral challenge was slavery, in the 20th century it was totalitarianism, and in this century it is the brutality inflicted on so many women and girls around the globe through human rights abuses such as sex trafficking or mass rape.[48]

It is widely reported that there are some 100 million "missing women" in the world.[49] While the ratio of men to women in the West is nearly even, in countries like China, India, and Pakistan, there are far fewer women than men.[50] This sex imbalance is attributed to, inter alia, sex-selection through abortion after a sonogram, malnutrition of female babies to better provide for sons, inadequate health care for female babies, and in some instances killing of female babies as a result of a state policy and a society that favors sons over daughters.

Certainly, the urging of Pope John XXIII affirming the rights and duties that belong to women as an aspect of their dignity must be

---

[47] *Supra* note 2, at 41.

[48] Nicholas D. Kristof and Sheryl WuDunn, *The Women's Crusade*, THE NEW YORK TIMES (Aug. 17, 2009), *http://www.nytimes.com/2009/08/23/magazine/23Women-t.html?pagewanted=all&_r=0.*

[49] *Id.*

[50] *Id.*

taken more seriously today as we confront these grave human rights abuses.

New Constitutions

Finally, we turn to the task of constitution-building and constitution-drafting. Today, as repressive governments are being replaced by whole new systems of governance, decisions such as the form, weight, structure, and functions of government must be made.

PACEM IN TERRIS offers guidance concerning the functions and requisites of good government.[51] First, the Encyclical notes that the chief concern of civil authorities must be to ensure that rights are recognized, respected, defended, and promoted.[52] Any government which *refused to recognize human rights or acted in violation of them, would not only fail in its duty; its decrees would be wholly lacking in binding force.*[53]

While the Encyclical does not advocate any particular form of government, such as a parliamentary system or a presidential system, a separation of powers is advised. A constitution that has clear rules defining the duties of public officials, as well as the rights and duties of citizens, is essential for good government, and the Common Good must always be the primary goal of government.

---

[51] *See* generally *Supra* note 2.

[52] *Supra* note 2, at 60.

[53] *Supra* note 2, at 61.

Most importantly, a constitution must contain a *clear and precisely worded charter of fundamental human rights.*[54] As new constitutions are drafted to replace those of the old regimes, let us hope that the principles outlined in PACEM IN TERRIS provide guidance.

Human rights are central to the mission of the United Nations. PACEM IN TERRIS makes an urgent plea on their behalf with regard to the United Nations. Pope John XXIII said:

> *May the day be not long delayed when every human being can find in [the United Nations] Organization an effective safeguard of one's personal rights; those rights, that is, which derive directly from one's dignity as a human person, and which are therefore universal, inviolable and inalienable.*[55]

In this dangerous and troubled age, we need to listen carefully to the words of Blessed John XXIII, and to take human rights seriously by always respecting the dignity of the human person.

---

[54] *Supra* note 2, at 75.

[55] *Supra* note 2, at 145.

7

PACEM IN TERRIS & ECONOMICS

Catholic Social Teaching on the Common Good versus the 'Austrian School' of Economics[1]

ANGUS SIBLEY

Fellow of the Institute of Actuaries (London)

Former Member of the London Stock Exchange and author of

THE "POISONED SPRING" OF LIBERTARIAN ECONOMICS

plus 90 articles published in USA, the UK, France, and Ireland

Order of Good Governance

O ne of the dominant themes of PACEM IN TERRIS is *order* because, as we read in its very first paragraph, peace on Earth depends upon *diligent observance of the divinely established order.* Accordingly, John XXIII sets out clearly and forcefully the basic importance and inestimable value of good government.

Quoting St Thomas' statement that *human law has the rationale of law insofar as it is in accordance with right reason, and as such it ob-*

---

viously derives from eternal law,[2] John observes that *authority must be exercised for the promotion of the common good. That is the primary reason for its existence.*[3]

John's encyclical thus stands in a long tradition of thinking about a very fundamental human concern: the need for good government, its priceless value to human society, and the difficult practical problem of how to establish and maintain it.

- In the Old Testament, King David speaks of the good and wise ruler: *he whose rule is upright on Earth, who rules in the fear of God, is like the morning light at sunrise.*[4]

- Aristotle tells us how *the state was first founded that we might live, but continued that we might live well.*[5]

- St John Chrysostom likewise: *for that there should be rulers ... and that all things should not just be carried on in confusion ... this, I say, is a work of God's wisdom.*[6]

- In our own times, Benedict XVI writes: *a just society must be the achievement of politics.*[7]

- At the opening of the Constitutional Convention in 1787, George Mason of Virginia wrote to his son: *the Eyes of the United States are turned upon this Assembly and their Expectations*

---

[2] SUMMA THEOLOGIAE I/II, Quest. 93, Art. 3

[3] PACEM IN TERRIS, N. 84

[4] 2 SAMUEL 23 :3

[5] POLITIKA, 1252b

[6] HOMILY 23 ON THE EPISTLE TO THE ROMANS

[7] DEUS CARITAS EST, N. 28

raised to a very anxious Degree. May God grant that we may be able to gratify them by establishing a wise and just Government.

Libertarian Rejection of Good Governance

But, from the standpoint of the 'Austrian' economists'[8] criticized in my book on the subject,[9] all the care and concern of the Founders of the American Republic, to establish a sound and beneficent federal State, were futile.

The most influential Austrian economists, Ludwig von Mises (1881-1979) and Friedrich von Hayek (1899-1992), lived through the era of Nazism and Communism. Such horrors convinced them that politics is inherently and incurably evil, that it is hardly possible for it to be made to serve the citizens of the *pólis* well. Therefore, they argued, let us take the economy out of politics. Let the economy be governed by the self-regulating market. In the words of a French critic, their philosophy *dissolves politics in economics.*[10]

- Hayek disparaged the very notion of the wise and beneficent exercise of political power; he claimed that, for individualists like himself, *power itself has always appeared the arch-evil.*[11] This

[8] In this text, 'Austrian' or 'Austrians' refers to economists of the 'Austrian school', not to citizens of Austria in general

[9] Angus Sibley, THE "POISONED SPRING" OF ECONOMIC LIBERTARIANISM: MENGER, MISES, HAYEK, ROTHBARD: A CRITIQUE FROM CATHOLIC SOCIAL TEACHING OF THE 'AUSTRIAN SCHOOL' OF ECONOMICS (Washington DC: Pax Romana Cmica-usa, 2011)

[10] Vincent Valentin, LES CONCEPTIONS NEO-LIBERALES DU DROIT, (Paris: Economica, 2002), p. 365

[11] THE ROAD TO SERFDOM (London: Routledge, 1944), Chap. 10

is like saying that electricity is intrinsically evil, because it is dangerous if it is not properly insulated and controlled.

- Mises stated that *freedom is to be found only in the sphere in which government does not interfere. Liberty is always freedom from the government.*[12]

- Hayek made the extraordinary claim that his ideal free-market society was *a social system that does not depend for its functioning on our finding good men for running it.*[13]

- The anarcho-capitalist Murray Rothbard even wrote that *if you wish to know how libertarians regard the state … simply think of the state as a criminal band.*[14]

How can we hope to achieve good government if attitudes like those dominate our thinking? Professor Timothy Snyder at Yale recently described Austrian economic thought as *inverted Marxism*;[15] just another vain longing for the state to wither away.

In the first pages of his most famous book, HUMAN ACTION, Mises unveiled his fundamental and startling rejection of an entire ethical tradition: in the past, he complained,

> *social problems were considered ethical problems. What were needed to construct the ideal society, they thought, were good*

---

[12] Lecture *Liberty and Property*, Princeton 1958 (reprinted Auburn, Alabama: The Ludwig von Mises Institute, 1991), in TWO ESSAYS BY LUDWIG VON MISES

[13] INDIVIDUALISM AND ECONOMIC ORDER (Chicago: University Press, 1948), p.12

[14] FOR A NEW LIBERTY, Second Edition (Auburn, Alabama: The Ludwig von Mises Institute, 2006), p. 57

[15] LE MONDE (Paris), 10 September 2012

princes and virtuous citizens. The discovery of the inescapable
interdependence of market phenomena overthrew this opinion.[16]

Thus, according to Mises, social problems are not primarily caused by people behaving badly; or by conflict between groups or classes with opposing interests and unequal bargaining powers; or by the ambitions of individuals clashing with the public interest.

No, the problems are caused by restrictions on our freedom as individuals to pursue in the marketplace whatever we may think are our own best interests. Hence, the only way to progress towards the ideal society is to allow individuals, pursuing their own ends, to interact freely in unhampered markets. That, rather than any ethical standard, should be our guiding principle.

The market must be allowed to impose its own law. According to Mises, the 'laws of economics' are like the laws of nature; they are universal laws, the same in all times and in all places; we can no more defy them than we can defy the laws of nature. *Nothing*, he says, *is left of economics if one denies the law of the market.*[17]

If you complain to a devotee of Austrian economics that free-market capitalism is needlessly harsh and unfair, he will likely accuse you of wishful thinking:

> *you may think it possible to organize a more equitable system,*
> *but it isn't; you are trying to go against the laws of nature. You*
> *cannot buck the market.*

---

[16] HUMAN ACTION (New Haven: Yale University Press, 1949), p. 2
[17] Ibid., p. 755

John's Critique of the Unordered Economy

John denounces this type of error: *many people,* he says,

> *think that the laws that govern persons' relations with the State are the same as those which regulate the blind, elemental forces of the Universe.*[18]

On the contrary, he says, politics, and economics too, must observe those divine laws which *clearly indicate how one must behave towards one's fellows in society.*[19]

In recent decades, we have gone far down Mises' road, which leads towards a society dominated not by elected government, but by markets. Are we happy with the consequences?

The deregulated market economy has brought us gaping inequalities, such as have not been seen since the 1900s. Traders in financial markets, heavily motivated by their immediate personal interests, bully and intimidate our businesses and even our governments, driving them to adopt unsound, short-sighted policies. Speculation in raw materials has brought violent instability in their prices, harming alternately producers and consumers.

Attainment of the Common Good, John tells us, *is the Purpose of the Public Authority.*[20] This phrase highlights another yawning gulf between Catholic teaching and Austrian economics, which explicitly rejects the concept of the Common Good, for two reasons.

---

[18] PACEM IN TERRIS, N. 6

[19] Ibid., N. 7

[20] Ibid., N. 53

Firstly, say Austrians, individuals and governments know little of what is best for the community; the market knows far better. For the market is the arena of interaction of all us individuals, each of us acting in our own personal interests; and this interaction reflects far more knowledge than is available to any one individual or to any institution, such as a City Hall or a government planning office.

That is doubtless true, but the market responds better to the whims of the affluent than to the needs of the poor; in politics we have *one person one vote*, while in the market we have *one dollar, one vote.* Moreover, with markets there is a curious paradox: **though they are indeed very knowledgeable, yet they are also grossly ignorant.**

For example, we as individuals know that we ought to restrain our consumption of petroleum, because it is a non-renewable resource whose use causes pollution. But the market, in effect, *does not know* these things; or at least, shall we say, it *behaves as if it does not know them.* The market motivates and even obliges us to burn oil rather than turn to renewable resources, because oil happens at present to be cheaper; if a business uses more costly energy sources, it will be uncompetitive and may not survive.

Secondly, if government obliges us, in the public interest, to do things that as individuals we might not choose to do, Austrian economists call this an intolerable intrusion upon our freedom. They say that because they think of freedom in negative and amoral terms. According to Hayek, freedom is simply *absence of restraint and constraint*[21] by the will of other people; elsewhere he wrote that *freedom is an opportunity to do good, but that is so only if it is also an opportunity to do wrong.*[22] Another free-market economist, Milton Friedman, held that *freedom has nothing to say about what an individual does with one's freedom.*[23]

By contrast, in Catholic teaching freedom is moral and positive: *there is no true freedom except in the service of what is good and just*, as the CATHOLIC CATECHISM[24] tells us. According to the modern Catholic theologian Bernard Häring, *in essence freedom is the power to do good ... the power to do evil is not of its essence.*[25] After all, in the New Testament sin is likened to slavery; so freedom is the opposite of sin. We cannot be truly free unless our conduct is in accord with the moral order.

It is interesting to note that a very similar view of freedom can be found in the Jewish tradition; thus the distinguished American theologian Rabbi Abraham Heschel (1907-1972) wrote that *one is free in doing good; one is not free in doing wrong. To do wrong is to fail to be free.*[26]

A well-ordered and peaceful society, says Pope John, *demands that people be guided by justice, respect the rights of others and do their du-*

---

[21] THE CONSTITUTION OF LIBERTY (London: Routledge & Kegan Paul, 1960), Chap. 1

[22] Ibid., Chap. 5

[23] CAPITALISM AND FREEDOM (Chicago: University Press, 1962), Introduction

[24] CATECHISM, N. 1733

[25] THE LAW OF CHRIST (Das Gesetz Christi, 1951), trans. E G Keyser (Cork: Mercier, 1961), Vol. I, Chap. 4

[26] THE INSECURITY OF FREEDOM (New York: Farrar, Strauss & Giroux, 1966), Part I, Chap. 1, Sect. 3

ty.[27] But in Austrian thinking, we have few rights apart from the 'right' to be left 'free' to *act according to coherent plans of our own,*[28] as Hayek put it. The notion of just prices and fair wages has no place in Austrian economic thought; the only correct price or wage is that which emerges in an unhampered market, and such a market is like a game in which *there is no sense in calling the outcome just or unjust.*[29]

An earlier Austrian economist, Carl Menger, observed that *a seamstress in Berlin, even if she works fifteen hours a day, cannot earn enough for her subsistence.*[30] Yet Menger had little time for agitators who wanted to see workers better paid; he accused them of *demanding nothing less than paying labor above its value.*[31] Menger's value of labor is not, as earlier classical economists used to say, enough pay for a worker to live on; it is whatever wage rate the market sets, reflecting consumer demand but unrelated to workers' needs.

Hayek insists that *'social justice' is an empty phrase with no determinable meaning,*[32] and complains that *the Roman Catholic Church has made the goal of social justice part of its official doctrine.*[33] Distributive justice is likewise rejected: *the results of an individual's efforts are*

---

[27] PACEM IN TERRIS, N. 35.

[28] THE CONSTITUTION OF LIBERTY, Chap. 1

[29] THE MIRAGE OF SOCIAL JUSTICE, vol. II of LAW, LEGISLATION & LIBERTY (Chicago: University Press, 1976), p.126

[30] PRINCIPLES OF POLITICAL ECONOMY (Grundsätze der Volkswirtschaftslehre, 1871), trans. Dingwall & Hoselitz (New York: University Press, 1976), p. 170

[31] Ibid., p. 174

[32] THE MIRAGE OF SOCIAL JUSTICE, p. 133

[33] Ibid., p. 66

necessarily unpredictable, and the question of whether the resulting dis-
tribution of income is just or unjust has no meaning.[34]

Compare John's statement:

> *A person has the inherent right not only to be given the oppor-*
> *tunity to work, but also to be allowed the exercise of personal*
> *initiative in the work one does ... the worker is entitled to a*
> *wage that is determined in accordance with the precepts of jus-*
> *tice.*[35]

Not simply by the amoral vagaries of the free market. On the subject of labor, the encyclical flies in the face of much currently-
fashionable theory and practice:

> *The government must make sure that workers are paid a just*
> *and equitable wage and are allowed a sense of responsibility in*
> *the industrial concerns for which they work.*[36]

This recalls John's earlier statement in MATER ET MAGISTRA:

> *A firm must not treat those employees ... as though they were*
> *mere cogs in the machinery ... keeping them merely passive in*
> *regard to decisions that regulate their activity.*[37]

In LABOREM EXERCENS, John Paul II also takes up this theme, calling for *sharing by the workers in the management and/or profits of busi-*
nesses, and arguing that each worker should be *fully entitled to con-*

---

[34] CONSTITUTION OF LIBERTY, p. 99

[35] PACEM IN TERRIS, N. 18

[36] Ibid., N. 64

[37] MATER ET MAGISTRA, N. 92

sider oneself a part-owner of the great workbench at which one is working with everyone else.[38]

In Europe, some countries have made real progress in that direction by setting up systems of 'co-determination' where workers have well-defined rights to participate in the direction of the businesses for which they work. In Germany, where this principle has been taken furthest, workers in large companies have the statutory right to elect 50% of the directors on a 'supervisory board' which determines basic company strategies.

PACEM IN TERRIS does not explicitly mention competition, except in a military context; but it does emphasize the right to association, with references back to MATER ET MAGISTRA and other encyclicals, which are eloquent on the need both for labor unions and for trade or professional associations.[39] These bodies have in principle the power, and indeed the purpose, of restraining excessive competition, though in the present climate they are often prevented from doing so.

> *The community constraint on competition is the means whereby the loser of competition avoids extinction, while the competitive winner is denied a clean sweep of the spoils of victory.*[40]

---

[38] LABOREM EXERCENS, N. 14

[39] MATER ET MAGISTRA was an earlier social encyclical letter of Blessed John XXIII, subtitled "On Christianity and Social Progress" and published in 1971 to commemorate the 70th anniversary of Leo's XIII's1981 social encyclical letter, RERUM NOVARUM. On this and other papal social encyclicals commemorating RERUM NOVARUM, see Joe Holland, 100 YEARS OF CATHOLIC SOCIAL TEACHING DEFENDING WORKERS AND THEIR UNIONS: SUMMARIES & COMMENTARIES FOR FIVE LANDMARK PAPAL ENCYCLICALS (Pacem in Terris Press, 2012).

[40] Allen & Hoekstra, TOWARDS A UNIFIED ECOLOGY, Chap. 6

That statement comes from a treatise on ecology and refers to plant and animal species; but it clearly fits human affairs pretty well too. We have been persuaded by free-marketeers that any restraint of competition is an economic sin; so, in many business sectors, we have virtually untrammeled competition.

It should be no surprise, then, that we have far too many individual losers who live in wretched conditions and become extinct rather quickly; while we also have competitive winners who sweep up huge spoils, but who hate the thought of paying taxes to assist those who come last in the fiercely competitive race.

Competition, in reality, is like certain hormones in the human body, which are necessary for health and survival, but pathogenic when present in excess. It is vitally important to get the hormonal balance right – in economics as well as in medicine.[41]

Need for Supranational Ordered Governance

In Part IV of PACEM IN TERRIS, John stresses the need for supranational order:

> The moral order itself demands the establishment of some general form of public authority ... equipped with worldwide power ... set up with the consent of all nations.[42]

Its role would be to promote the worldwide common good in matters of economics, society, politics and culture.

---

[41] Angus Sibley, *The Hyperthyroid Economy*, JOURNAL OF THE ROYAL SOCIETY OF MEDICINE (London), June 1995, accessible on *www.equilibrium-economicum.net*.

[42] PACEM IN TERRIS, N. 137 - 138

In today's postcolonial world, one may well say that the only remaining supranational powers with real clout are the financial markets. And those markets clearly need restraint and discipline, which can scarcely be provided by national governments; for international markets tend to escape their control.

In Europe, we are having to establish stronger supranational regulation to stop capricious bond markets from ruining individual countries. *The primacy of politics over the financial markets must be reestablished,*[43] said Angela Merkel recently. Happily, this urgent need is pushing us towards the development of effective international order.

If Pope John could return to Earth today, what would he think of our present situation? He would be glad to see that we have moved away from the Cold War confrontation, cut back our nuclear arsenals, and moved a little closer to recognizing the supremacy of international law. But he would surely be sadly disappointed with our economic behavior.

When John wrote PACEM IN TERRIS, we had economies in which one could generally find a job without undue difficulty; in which democracies were not constantly at the mercy of speculative markets; in which we were not plagued by excessive competitive stresses. Since then, we have achieved substantial economic growth which, however, has principally benefited a very few at the top; and we have reached a situation where pollution and climate change threaten to lead to catastrophe, where the human race as a whole is consuming natural resources at unsustainable rates.

---

[43] Bundestag, May 5 2010

Researchers estimate that overall consumption in the USA is now so extravagant that, if the whole human race lived in American style, we would need four planets to provide sufficient natural resources.[44] And yet, according to 2011 figures[45] from the US Department of Agriculture, 50 million Americans – almost 16% of the population – live in "food-insecure households," meaning that they suffer malnutrition or hunger.

It appears that the current American economic system is very good – indeed, all too good – at maximizing production and consumption; but incapable of distributing the goods fairly and reasonably. Yet, I repeat, according to Hayek, *the question of whether the distribution of income is just or unjust has no meaning.*

Why do many continue to revere economists like Hayek? Because they are living, just like our former opponents the communists, under a grand economic delusion.

Austrian economics, and indeed free-market economics in general, has played a big part in our recent growth in overconsumption, unemployment, and poverty. We can trace this problem right back to Adam Smith, who seemed more concerned with boosting production and consumption than with giving the workers a fair deal.

Smith argued that, if we abolished the craft guilds, then craftsmen's profits and their employees' wages would all be lower, *but the public would be a gainer, the work of all artificers coming in this way*

---

[44] WWF LIVING PLANET REPORT 2012, 43

[45] See *www.ers.usda.gov/media/884525/err141.pdf*, page 16

much cheaper to market.[46] Apparently, Smith did not see craftsmen and their employees as being part of the public!

This kind of economics has always been on the side of the consumer who wants to buy more of everything cheaper; always biased against the worker struggling to earn a decent living. It is justified by the theory that the economy exists only to satisfy the needs and desires of consumers; that work is merely a necessary evil that has to be done in order to produce what we consume.

But work is more than just a factor of production. A leading German economist, Gustav Schmoller, who fought a long-running battle against the Austrian economists, observed that *man cannot do nothing but eat and make love, he needs other things to occupy his time and his soul … all moral strength has its roots in work.*[47]

Economists today have little regard for Schmoller, who has never been translated into English. We have other priorities, such as *labor productivity* (producing more with less human labor): *Obsessed with productivity, we strive never with six to do the work of five.*

But this means John's ideal, that everyone should have opportunities to work, cannot be realized unless we continue to produce and consume ever more and more of everything. Mother Nature, I am afraid, will not permit that to continue indefinitely.

In Adam Smith's day, world population was about one-tenth of its present level; most people had very low standards of living, but

---

[46] WEALTH OF NATIONS, Book I, Chap. 9, Part 2

[47] GRUNDRISS DER ALLGEMEINEN VOLKSWIRTSCHAFTSLEHRE, vol. I (Leipzig: Duncker & Humblot, 1900), pp. 21 and 39

there was little pressure on natural resources. So an economic phi-losophy that promoted endless growth was not entirely unreason-able. Today, we need to recognize that this kind of economics is obsolete.

Japanese economist Naoshi Yamawaki, professor at the University of Tokyo, notes that the neoclassical school of economics, the 'Chicago school',

> *... deals with the ethical dimension of the economy merely from the viewpoint of efficiency and that Austrian economics shares with neoclassical economics this ethical negligence.*[48]

That is a very serious charge; and there can be little doubt that the verdict must be Guilty.

We have adopted as our guideline for economic and business strategy an ideology that is amoral and ethically negligent. There lies the root cause of our current economic miseries. Yet all this does not mean that capitalism is fundamentally rotten.

If economists would talk to electrical engineers, they might learn that there is a type of electric motor, traditionally used in street-cars and subway trains, that has a curious peculiarity: when it is not attached to the wheels of a train, not constrained by the train's inertia, it must never be allowed to run free on full power.[49] For in those circumstances it has a natural tendency to accelerate without limit till its rotating center flies apart. That does not mean that the

---

[48] *Walter Eucken and Wilhelm Röpke*, in THE GERMAN HISTORICAL SCHOOL (London & New York: Routledge, 2001), p. 198

[49] Angus Sibley, *Free Markets easily spin out of control*, INTERNATIONAL HERALD TRIBUNE, 13 May 1998; accessible on *www.equilibrium-economicum.net*

motor is faulty. It simply means that it can function only under constraint.

The capitalist economy is like that motor. Without adequate constraints, it runs amok, destroying itself and human society too. So it is time for us to awake from the free-marketeers' dream, or rather nightmare, of markets running free from democratic (with a small "d") political control. That is a recipe for financial, social and ecological disaster.

Catholic social and economic teaching provides many insights and guidelines to steer us away from the grave errors of libertarian capitalism. But this is an aspect of Catholic doctrine that is too little known and too seldom proclaimed with sufficient vigor. We need much stronger emphasis on this vitally important body of teaching, both to help our societies out of their current economic impasse, and to give the Church renewed credibility and relevance.

Conclusion:
A Different Austrian Vision

Finally, a quick anecdote. Austrian economists are hostile to labor unions and to industrial democracy; Hayek insisted that *unions are the prime source of unemployment.*[50] But the Republic of Austria has flagrantly ignored their advice. It has a social-market economy like that of Germany, with strong unions, predominant collective bargaining, and widespread worker representation on company supervisory boards.

---

[50] UNEMPLOYMENT AND THE UNIONS (London: Institute of Economic Affairs, 1980), p. 52

The result? Austria is among the richest countries in Europe; and its unemployment rate, at around 4%, is among the lowest in Europe.

8

PACEM IN TERRIS & PHILOSOPHY

The Encyclical's Stoic Vision of Global Order
versus Modern Ideologies Rooted in Epicurean Chaos[1]

JOE HOLLAND, PH.D.

President, Pax Romana / Catholic Movement for Intellectual & Cultural Affairs - USA

Professor of Philosophy & Religion, St. Thomas University in Miami Gardens, Florida

Your Excellencies Archbishop Chullikatt and Ambassador Shafer, Dr. Corden, Dean Defeis, Mr. Sibley, distinguished guests, ladies and gentlemen: I bring you greetings from the directors and members of Pax Romana / Catholic Movement for Intellectual and Cultural Affairs - USA, and from the leadership of our core project, the Pacem in Terris Global Leadership Ecumenical Initiative.[2]

Also, in the name of our directors and members, I thank Archbishop Chullikatt and the Permanent Observer Mission of the Holy See to the United Nations, as well as Ambassador Shafer and the Permanent Observer Mission of the Sovereign Military Order of Malta to the United Nations, for convening this important event.

---

[1] Copyright © Joe Holland 2012

[2] For more information on this Initiative, see *http://paceminterris.net.*

In addition, thank you to the two leaders of our Pax Romana CMI-CA-USA New York Office for the United Nations, namely Dr. Josef Klee and Ambassador Francis Dubois, and our then St. Thomas University School of Law intern at the Office, Ms. Alejandra Rosero, as well as the generous volunteers helping the Office, especially Ms. Maria Almeida. Through their work on behalf of the Office's "Pax Romana at the UN" project, they have done an important service for the United Nations and for the human family.

Introduction

The fiftieth anniversary of Pope John XXIII's famous 1963 encyclical letter, PACEM IN TERRIS, occurs in April of 2013. But it is fitting that this Symposium, gathering in 2012, now prepares for this important anniversary. It is especially fitting because this very month when the Symposium gathers, October of 2012, marks the 50th Anniversary of the infamous Cuban Missile Crisis.

Over that event, there hung – like an apocalyptic sword – the terrifying threat of global nuclear war. Such a war would probably have caused across the globe the death of hundreds of millions of human lives. It would also have inflicted incalculable damage on the beauteous and fragile ecosystem of creatures in the Creator's beloved Earth Community. That threat of global thermonuclear war reportedly moved John to publish this, his most famous encyclical letter.

Participants have already been provided a copy of my small book prepared especially for this Symposium. As the book's title indicates, it offers a detailed summary of and commentary on the encyclical.[3] So this presentation will not repeat the book's task. Instead, it will address the document's underlying philosophical dimension. At the heart of this dimension stand two deep claims.

- The first deep claim is that PACEM IN TERRIS's call for global governance of the emerging global human society reflects the classical Catholic appropriation of the Roman Stoics' philosophical view of human society as called to order itself, just as the divinely governed Cosmos has its own magnificent order.

- The second deep claim is that, by continuing the Stoic philosophical doctrine of the need for human order to echo the cosmic order, PACEM IN TERRIS fundamentally rejects the two dominant modern industrial ideologies. For these ideologies have been grounded in a chaotic interpretation of the Universe, which sees everything moved only by blind and random chance without any rational order – as taught by the ancient Greek materialist philosopher Epicurus (341-270 BCE).

This presentation on the philosophical dimension of PACEM IN TERRIS is divided into four parts:

- *Context:* the document's historical context, found especially in the Cuban Missile Crisis

- *Critique:* its philosophical critique of the two modern ideologies which led to that crisis, again with those ideologies rooted in the philosophical errors of Epicurean materialism

---

[3] Joe Holland, PACEM IN TERRIS: SUMMARY & COMMENTARY FOR THE 50TH ANNIVERSARY OF THE FAMOUS ENCYCLICAL LETTER OF POPE JOHN XXIII ON WORLD PEACE (Pacem in Terris Press, 2012). It may be purchased though a link found in the "Books" page of the website for the Pacem in Terris Global Leadership Ecumenical Initiative: *http://paceminterris.net/Books.html.*

- *Vision:* the encyclical's rich philosophical vision of human order, rooted in the classical Stoic philosophy of a divinely inspired cosmic order – the alternative which it proposes to the modern ideologies grounded in the Epicurean philosophy

- *Significance:* its prophetic significance for then, and more so for now

The second part of this presentation will be the lengthiest, with the other three briefer.

Context: The Cuban Missile Crisis and the Crisis of Modern Ideologies

The Cuban Missile Crisis constituted the most dangerous point in the late modern Cold War. Its threat to human life, and to all life within our Earth Community, called into question the foundational philosophy undergirding the two dominant ideologies of the modern industrial civilization, namely Liberal Capitalism and Scientific Socialism.

It is necessary to explore this foundational philosophy, because since John XXIII we find in contemporary Catholic Social Teaching a call to move beyond the two dominant ideologies of modern industrial civilization, which its sees as incapable of developing a *true* world order – due to common philosophical errors.

From the time of Leo XIII (pope from 1878 to 1903) but prior to Blessed John XXIII (elected in 1958), the strategy of "Modern Catholic Social Teaching" had been fundamentally opposed to the industrial ideology of Scientific Socialism, but it had sought to reform the industrial ideology of Liberal Capitalism into support for a modern form of Western Christian Civilization.⁴ From John XXIII forward, however, a new "Postmodern Catholic Social Teaching" now seeks to help guide the human family beyond the philosophical errors of both dominant modern ideologies.⁵

---

⁴ For a review of the modern strategy, see Joe Holland, MODERN CATHOLIC SOCIAL TEACHING: THE POPES CONFRONT THE INDUSTRIAL AGE 1740-1958 (Paulist Press, 2003).

⁵ In the tradition of Catholic Social Teaching, the term "Capitalism" has been treated in various ways. Early on, for example, it is often referred to simply as "Liberalism."

In his 1891 social encyclical RERUM NOVARUM, Leo XIII sought to reform Laissez-Faire Capitalism by supporting workers' unions and a regulatory state, but also – and essentially – by changing its philosophical foundation (which never happened). In his 1991 social encyclical CENTESIMUS ANNUS, John Paul II noted that the term "Capitalism" has different meanings, and he preferred instead the phrase "Business Economy." Of course, business is thousands of years older than "Liberal Capitalism" and, if there is to be a new post-capitalist era in the future, certainly the "Business Economy" will still be central to that future.

In any case, what Catholic Social Teaching criticizes at the most fundamental level is what it sees as the erroneous philosophy at the theoretical foundation of Liberal Capitalism, which philosophy it then sees as the source of Liberal Capitalism's social and ecological (and spiritual) problems. While Catholic Social Teaching certainly criticizes greed and injustice, especially as expressions of human "sin," it nonetheless sees the philosophical errors underlying Liberal Capitalism as the basic cause of the modern explosion of these "sins."

Similarly, the term "Socialism" has different meanings in this tradition. While in the second half of the 19ᵗʰ century Marx and Engels gained ideological hegemony on the left for "Scientific Socialism," prior to Marx and Engels wide sectors of the socialist movement were described as "Christian Socialism" – a movement which had nothing to do with Marxism since it was prior to Marxism. Marx and Engels were even required to wage an intellectual war against the existing movement known as "Christian Socialism" before their "Scientific Socialism" could achieve its ideological hegemony. Indeed, much later, John XXIII as a young priest still held to the notion of "Christian Socialism."

Also, in his 1931 social encyclical QUADRAGESIMO ANNO, Pius XI even noted that in many ways "moderate Socialism" (equivalent today to "Social Democra-

This postmodern strategy of Catholic Social Teaching, inaugurated by John, does not any long support the idea of Christian Civilization. Instead, it calls for a new global civilization which will not be specifically Christian, but rather broadly humanistic and also ecological (and thereby implicitly supporting the values of Catholic Social Teaching). Further, in the creation of this new global civilization, it calls for creative contributions from all the great spiritual traditions of the human family, as well as from people of good will.[6]

This new critique of both dominant modern industrial ideologies, which takes on subtle but pervasive power in PACEM IN TERRIS, is essential for truly understanding the depth of this document. Without this deep philosophical understanding, we find only a surface reading.

---

cy") was similar to Catholic Social Teaching (described then as "Christian Democracy"). The main difference between the two, he argued, was in the materialist and atheistic philosophy still undergirding the secular movement known as "moderate socialism."

Further, in his 1981 social encyclical LABOREM EXERCENS, John Paul argued that Marxism did not really achieve its goal of politically and economically empowering workers, and instead simply turned political-economic power over to the centralized state (which John Paul then described in CENTESIMUS ANNUS as "State Capitalism"). And so he called for society to achieve what Marxism failed to achieve, namely true worker participation in the political economy – certainly through unions, but even more through cooperatives and workers sharing in management and ownership.

Overall, therefore, we might say that Catholic Social Teaching supports the true insights of what might be called "reformed Capitalism" and "moderate Socialism," but not the erroneous philosophical foundations of either of the two dominant ideologies of Liberal Capitalism or Scientific Socialism.

[6] On this new strategy, see my soon to be published book THE VISION OF JOHN XXIII: PROPHETIC FOUNDER OF CATHOLIC SOCIAL TEACHING FOR THE POSTMODERN GLOBAL ERA (forthcoming from Pacem in Terris Press in 2013).

John's code word for this philosophical dimension is *truth* – Divine truth, the truth of the Cosmos, the truth of the Earth's ecosystem, and the truth of humanity within it – all gently set against the philosophical *errors* of reductionist and materialist modern ideologies. Thus, the encyclical's subtitle is: ON ESTABLISHING UNIVERSAL PEACE IN *TRUTH*, JUSTICE, LOVE, AND LIBERTY (italics added).

The result of these *errors*, John argued, is a fundamental crisis of modern industrial civilization which came to a head during the Cuban Missile Crisis in the apocalyptic threat of nuclear war. The root cause of this crisis, as proposed in PACEM IN TERRIS, is competitive ideological nationalisms lacking a true philosophy of global order designed to serve the global common good.

Critique: Philosophical Errors
of Modern Ideologies

Surface Roots in Modern European Enlightenment

Early on, as noted, the underlying philosophical assumptions of modern industrial civilization divided into the two antagonistic (yet commonly reductionist and materialist) ideologies of Liberal Capitalism and Scientific Socialism. Since Pope Leo XIII's 1891 landmark encyclical, RERUM NOVARUM,[7] and still today, Catholic Social Teaching has argued that both of these modern ideologies grew out of errors of the *philosophes* of the modern European Enlightenment (despite the Enlightenment's many good points, and

---

[7] *http://www.vatican.va/holy_father/leo_xiii/encyclicals/documents/hf_l-xiii_enc_15051891_rerum-novarum_en.html.* (Accessed 2012-10-15.) Leo served as pope from 1878 to 1903.

also despite valid insights within each of the two modern ideologies).

Catholic Social Teaching has especially argued that both modern ideologies, despite their antagonism, share common philosophical errors (again, from the Enlightenment) about the nature of the human. These errors may be stated as follows.

- *Liberal Capitalism.* Celebrating the theme of "freedom," Liberal Capitalism's ideology has emphasized the more empirically oriented individualism of the Enlightenment's Scottish-English side, and in so doing has undermined authentic human community and tried to reduce the human person to an autonomous fragment subordinate to "market-efficiency."

- *Scientific Socialism.* Meanwhile, celebrating the theme of "solidarity," Scientific-socialism's ideology has emphasized the more rationally oriented collectivism of the Enlightenment's French-German side, and in so doing has also undermined authentic human community and tried to collapse the human person into an impersonal collectivity subordinate to "state-power."

In addition, to reflect beyond the timeframe of PACEM IN TERRIS, we may note that both modern industrial systems have been undermining ecological community (on which our human family and all other creatures depend for survival). Further, both ideologies have, in different ways, been promoting an increasingly secularized and materialist worldview.

Currently, the worst features of both modern industrial ideologies seem to be joining together, as seen in the growing anti-democratic cooperation between economic elites of Global Capitalism and political elites of Communist China. Already, this alliance seems to be producing a negative late modern "merger" between what Pope Pius XI in his 1931 social encyclical letter QUADRAGESIMO ANNO (published to commemorate the 40th anniversary of RERUM NOVARUM) called *economic dictatorship* (Liberal Capitalism) and *political dictatorship* (Scientific Socialism). But adequately exploring this "merger" would take us beyond the framework of PACEM IN TERRIS.

Deep Roots in Epicurean Philosophy

Both of these modern industrial ideologies, again Liberal Capitalism and Scientific Socialism, find their deep roots in the earlier modern European Scientific Revolution, called at the time the "New Science." Founders of that New Science like Isaac Newton (1642-1747) were called at the time not "scientists" but "natural philosophers",[8] and they based their philosophical understanding of the Universe on the atomistic-mechanical doctrine of Epicurus.[9]

---

[8] Newton's 1687 scientific masterpiece was titled PHILOSOPHIAE NATURALIS PRINCIPIA MATHEMATICA (Mathematical Principles of Natural Philosophy).

[9] The early modern Western scientific appropriation of the philosophy of Epicurus is not widely understood either by the contemporary Western scientific community or by the contemporary Western philosophical community. For recent scholarship on this matter, see the broadly researched and lyrically written book by Catherine Wisdom, EPICUREANISM AT THE ORIGIN OF MODERNITY (Oxford University Press, 2010). Wilson, a Canadian scholar, is Regius Professor of Moral Philosophy at the University of Aberdeen in Scotland. See also the delightfully told tale of the early modern recovery and appropriation of the Roman philosopher-poet Lucretius' classic work on Epicurus, DE RERUM NATURA. This second book, by Harvard's famous Shakespeare scholar, Stephen Goldblatt, is titled THE SWERVE: HOW THE WORLD BECAME MODERN (W.W. Norton, 1912). The "swerve" is an important theme in Epicurus' materialist

Epicureanism was one of the major classical Greek philosophical schools competing for attention in the Hellenistic culture ushered in by Aristotle's famous pupil, the young Macedonian conqueror Alexander the Great (356-323 BCE).

Epicurus held that everything in the Universe, and the Universe itself, could be reduced to small uncuttable particles of matter (too small for the eye to see) called *atoma* (in Greek meaning "uncuttable," with the singular being *atomos* and translated into English as "atom"). He saw these "atoms" moving blindly and chaotically by their own individual force, like so many individual wills lacking rational mind, with all randomly swerving within the vortex of an empty void.

For Epicurus, the Universe was not truly *Cosmos* (meaning in Greek an intelligible "order"), but only the *chaos* (meaning in Greek lack of order) of blind materialism. He saw the "atoms" as accidentally forming temporary aggregates, with the sum of these aggregates blindly and temporarily constituting everything in the Universe. Over time, according to Epicurus, these aggregates by chance began to function mechanically. He then saw the overarching mechanical sum of all lesser aggregates as the accidental and temporary structure of the Universe.

Epicurus' mechanical Universe did not constitute a true unity with rational order. For, according to him, there was no logical relation-

---

philosophy. Both Wilson and Goldblatt appear to support the Epicurean materialist worldview, and Goldblatt unfortunately reveals a stereotypically modernist ignorance of the classical Catholic intellectual tradition. Nonetheless, both books are works of valuable scholarship.

ship among the parts, only aggregation by material force, with all eventually doomed to collapse into materialist disaggregation.

Thus, Epicurus claimed that our Universe is without what John XXIII called the *truth* of rational order. For him, it was only a random and chaotic ongoing process of atomistic-mechanical aggregation and disaggregation, structured only by the random and temporary chance of blind force. In this materialist cosmology, Epicurus argued, our human existence and all of reality are meaningless.

Epicurus admitted, however, that we humans do have a rational mind, but he saw human reason as having no substantive purpose. It could only be used, he claimed, to perform an instrumental utilitarian calculus of pleasure and pain. Using reason only instrumentally – to minimize pain and to seek modest pleasures – was the narrow task of his philosophical ethics. (This is the classical philosophical root of modern Western utilitarian ethics.)

Further, finding no rational meaning in reality, Epicurus "ethically" encouraged his followers to abandon political life, to shun marriage and children, to treat sexuality as a compulsive source of pleasure with no significance for relationships, and to withdraw with a few close friends into a private "garden" (as he had done). There, he argued, one should seek to reduce pain, perhaps be consoled with modest pleasures, reject religion as only a source of fear, and eventually accept death without fear, since there will no longer be any consciousness after one's "atoms" disaggregate.

In sum, the Epicurean philosophy and its ethics are atomistic-mechanical and reductionist-materialist. As we will now see, this philosophy became the cosmological foundation of the early modern West's "New Science."

Philosophical Reductionism of Modern Science

The atomistic-mechanical and so reductionist-materialist Epicurean philosophy was chosen by early modern European "natural philosophers" (again, today called "scientists"[10]) as the cosmological foundation for "Particle Physics," and later for "Molecular Chemistry" and still later for "Molecular Biology."

Most recently, and again following the Epicurean atomistic-mechanical paradigm, some scientists have applied its materialist reductionism to genetics, as we see with the so-called "selfish gene" of Richard Dawkins. Promoting a militant atheism, Dawkins portrays the gene as the biological "atom" which supposedly determines and explains biological evolution, and thus leaves human life without authentic free will or spiritual meaning.[11]

---

[10] Use of the word "scientist" did not become common until the 19th Century. The word "scientist" is from the Latin word *scientia,* which means "knowledge." Hence, literally, "scientist" means one with knowledge (or pursuing knowledge). But, of course, this is true of many other intellectual professions.

[11] Richard Dawkins, a British zoologist and professor at Oxford University, is a leading propagandist in the philosophical school of the so-called "New Atheism." His arguments, and those of the "New Atheist" school in general, are restatements of classical Epicurean philosophy set within a neo-Darwinian interpretation of evolution. See, for example, his books THE SELFISH GENE: THIRTIETH ANNIVERSARY EDITION (Oxford University Press, 2006) and THE GOD DELUSION (Mariner Books, Reprint Edition, 2008). For a different and more holistic and richer interpretation of biological science, grounded in recent discoveries and open to spirituality, see physicist Fritjof Capra's THE WEB OF LIFE: A NEW UNDERSTANDING OF LIVING SYSTEMS (Anchor Books, 1997).

But for early "natural philosophers" there was a problem. Epicurus had been militantly anti-religious, yet the early modern European scientists were generally Christians – Catholics, Anglicans, and Protestants, with a few Deists.[12] So how could they have accepted anti-religious Epicurean materialism as the philosophical foundation of their New Science?

The answer is that those great early modern Christian scientists thought that they could dualistically combine Epicurus' materialist "natural philosophy" with a purely transcendent understanding of "supernatural theology," be it in voluntarist form from William of Ockham's Nominalism or in the rationalist form of the Renaissance's Neo-Platonist philosophy (which eventually renamed Plato's "demiurge," whom he saw as the craftsman or architect of the *Cosmos*, as the Divine "watchmaker" who supposedly designed a purely mechanical Universe and then left it to run by itself).

In this dualism, the purely "spiritual" Creator was seen as having designed and created a purely "material" Universe devoid of any spiritual presences and functioning in a purely atomistic-mechanical fashion.

On the one hand, the "materialist" side of this philosophical dualism then became the foundational paradigm for modern Western science, including the supposedly scientific disciplines of politics

---

[12] For example, Isaac Newton was deeply religious. While pretending to be an Anglican and even required by Oxford University to continue (until his death) as a candidate for Anglican ordination, he was in fact what would be called today a "Unitarian." Further, Newton was deeply interested in esoteric religious traditions and, as has been recently discovered, his religious writings in "natural theology" constitute a larger corpus than his scientific writings in "natural philosophy."

and economics, and for the common atomistic-mechanical and reductionist-materialist understanding of science in both Liberal-Capitalism and Scientific-Socialism.

On the other hand, human access to the "spiritual" side of the dualism came to be seen as only psychological, as established in the modern revision of Platonism developed in the philosophy of René Descartes (1596-1650), who still today is known as the "father" of modern Western philosophy.[13]

The early modern Cartesian revision of Platonic dualism found popular resonance in the highly psychologized late medieval bourgeois Christian "spirituality," seen initially in emotionally oriented Protestant "pietism" and Catholic "devotionalism" – both significantly disconnected from consciousness of Divine presence within nature and history. More generally, this modern bourgeois form has been described as the spirituality of "interiority," defined early on as the *Devotio Moderna* (modern devotionalism), though with roots going back to the Neo-Platonism of St. Augustine.[14]

---

[13] What distinguished Descartes' modernized Platonism from the classical view of Plato was that Descartes saw the Universe as atomistic and mechanical and devoid of spiritual meaning, whereas Plato had seen it as a reflection or image of Divine beauty and order. Thus, for Plato the beauty of the Universe lead to knowledge of Divine Beauty. For Descartes, however, the two were fundamentally different and disconnected.

[14] See Owen C. Thomas, "Interiority and Christian Spirituality," THE JOURNAL OF RELIGION, Vol. 80, No. 1 (Jan., 2000), pp. 41-60. It is interesting that perhaps the most significant Catholic expression of modern Western spirituality is found in the "Spiritual Exercises" of St. Ignatius of Loyola, which have a strong psychological character. But Ignatian spirituality still breaks beyond bourgeois psychological limitations.

This spiritual reductionism limited the Divine Mystery to pure transcendence, in turn to be experienced by humans only psychologically, and rejecting any awareness of the immanent Divine presence revealed in nature and history. Thus, within the modern framework, this inner "subjective" reductionism of modern bourgeois psychological spirituality dualistically complemented the outer "objective" reductionism of modern bourgeois materialist science.

But, beginning with Sigmund Freud (1856-1939), this psychologized spirituality would be undermined by the triumph of reductionist materialism in scientific psychology. As a result, for many bourgeois Christians, spirituality first became privatized and then collapsed into secularized materialist psychology.

Similarly, the modern Western scientific university increasingly accepted the modern secular definition of reality as purely materialist, with spiritual meaning at first marginalized and then denied. Logically, then, the university's definition of knowledge became instrumentally reduced to the quantification of mathematics, with the statistics of "metrics" becoming foundational, yet at the same time empty of any substantive philosophical meaning.

This tendency to reduce knowledge to an instrumental utilitarian calculus was also a fruit of the Florentine Renaissance, which had resurrected Plato's doctrine that mathematics is the highest form of linguistically articulated knowledge. But, whereas Plato's mathematics had drawn him away from the material world toward "higher" spiritual truth, mathematics after the Renaissance pointed away from any spiritual truth toward reductionist materialism. Eventually, it made the quantification of money the "bottom line" of everything. (This may not be surprising, since the Medicis, great patrons of the Florentine Renaissance, were powerful international bankers.)

Thus, claiming to be grounded in modern science and eliminating for their science any spiritual dimension, the two dominant modern materialist ideologies – again, Liberal Capitalism and Scientific Socialism – both pursued as their highest value quantified economic growth, measured only by the abstraction of money. Such materialist growth became the mathematical idol of both ideologies, though they have differed on how to pursue it.

- On one side, the liberal-capitalist ideology has sought utilitarian monetarized growth through the blind voluntarism of the "free-market."

- On the other side, the scientific-socialist ideology has sought utilitarian monetarized growth through the secular rationalism of the "socialist state."[15]

---

[15] Marxism, with its centralizing of power in the state, appears rationalist and not Epicurean. But, for Marx, the rationalist role of the socialist state was only an instrumentally utilitarian means for overcoming economic scarcity. Once that scarcity was overcome and full "communism" was achieved, Marx thought that the state would "wither away." Everyone would then supposedly become a completely "free individual" – like an Epicurean atom. Thus, Marxism, though instrumentally rationalist (as is Epicureanism), ultimately seeks not the rationally ordered Stoic *Cosmos* but rather the empty, atomized, and economistically libertarian "freedom" of Epicurean *Chaos*. So, while Liberal Capitalism and Scientific Socialism disagree about the means to get there, both agree that the ultimate goal is a rationally utilitarian and spiritually empty libertarian "freedom" of the individual. By contrast, Catholic Social Teaching has seen such so-called "freedom" as a common and fundamental philosophical *error* of both modern economistic ideologies.

But only with the late modern communications revolution (radio, cinema, TV, and Internet) has the reductionist-materialist paradigm of Epicurus' atomistic-mechanistic philosophy finally, and on a mass scale, colonized the Western cultural consciousness and the cultural consciousness of others wherever modern Western consumerism triumphs.

Now – at the end of the 500-year cycle of the modern Western historical project, which has been scientifically grounded in Epicurean philosophy – we increasingly see the psychological triumph of self-centered individualism, the political and economic erosion of rooted organic human-ecological community, and the cultural-spiritual collapse of meaning into a sterile and increasingly destructive scientific-technological secularism, which may even be pointing in a neo-totalitarian direction.

Smith and Marx as Epicurean Philosophers

The two foundational thinkers for the two dominant modern industrial ideologies were Adam Smith (1723-1790) and Karl Marx (1818-1883). Both were both philosophers. The Scottish philosopher Smith had studied philosophy first at the University of Glasgow and later at Oxford. The German philosopher Marx had completed his doctorate in philosophy at the University of Berlin. As philosophers theoretizing about human society, both Smith and Marx grounded their theories in Epicurus.

Adam Smith, drawing on the modern European Enlightenment's British empiricist and individualistic side, appropriated the Epicurean atomistic-mechanical philosophy from the physics of "Newtonian Mechanics," and also from the intense philosophical Epicureanism of his friend David Hume (1711-1776). He then used

Newtonian physics to explain the "free market" as the blind movement of supposedly atomized human individuals guided only by the utilitarian calculus of autonomous "self-interest."[16]

A century later, the young doctoral student Marx became initially steeped in the idealist dialectical rationalism of G.W.F. Hegel (1770-1831). But, against Hegel's original idealism, he embraced the rebellious atheistic materialism of the later left-wing Hegelians, to which he joined the atomistic-mechanical philosophy of Epicurus. Marx then enthusiastically wrote his doctoral dissertation on Epicurus, with praise for his philosophical system.

Later, Marx founded what he called "Scientific Socialism" by combining his atheistic-materialist interpretation of the Hegelian dialectic with his rebellious appropriation of the atomistic-mechanical philosophy of Epicurus, as appropriated by early modern science in Newtonian physics (thus the adjective "Scientific" in Marx's ideology).[17]

---

[16] This was tempered, however, by Smith's simultaneous embrace of the Stoic teaching about virtue (also true of Hume). But for Smith (as for Hume), virtue was seen as subjective, and his embrace of the Epicurean materialist doctrines for the objective world remained more fundamental, with Epicurean *chaos* thus negating Stoic *Cosmos* in his purely voluntarist doctrine of the "free-market."

[17] Just as Marx saw the atomized capitalist owners joining together as a social class into a "mass" force against the workers, so too he saw the atomized workers becoming revolutionary when they were collectivized into the larger "mass" of the proletariat, which then would then have greater physical force than the capitalists. For Marx, class conflict thus was understood "scientifically" (again meaning through Newtonian physics) as the conflict of two mass forces, with the larger mass force of the workers eventually overcoming the smaller mass force of the capitalists. But then Marx used the Hegelian dialectic to propose that the worker's victorious outcome would not be simply that, but rather also

Catholic Social Teaching's Critique
of Both Materialist Ideologies

As John XXIII argued in PACEM IN TERRIS and as Catholic Social Teaching has argued since Leo XIII, the two modern Western materialist ideologies of Liberal Capitalism and Scientific Socialism are in the same erroneous philosophical family with similar philosophical errors.

One major result of these philosophical errors, as popes after Leo argued, was that the competition of modern industrial nations, lacking any philosophical vision of rational order for international society, led to "world wars." Further, as John later argued in PACEM IN TERRIS, such national competition has now confronted us with the threat of global thermonuclear devastation. Such is the fundamental philosophical crisis of modern industrial civilization, which lacks a rational philosophy of global order.

In light of this terminal crisis of modern industrial civilization, we now turn to John's alternative vision for human civilization.

John's Prophetic Vision for
the New Global Era

Early Christian Appropriation of Stoicism

In contrast to the Epicurean vision of blind *Chaos* at the philosophical root of the two modern industrial ideologies, John's vision in PACEM IN TERRIS is rooted in the alternative philosophical school

---

the creation of a new form of society, namely "Scientific Socialism". This proposal was based on Hegel's dialectical principle that at a certain point an increase in quantitative change becomes a qualitative change.

which competed with Epicureanism to shape Western Civilization during the Hellenistic period. That is classical Roman Stoicism, which early Christianity embraced and adapted to its own use.

Early Christian thinkers rejected Epicureanism, understandably so because it was purely materialist and anti-religious. Instead, they looked favorably on the Stoic philosophy (though modifying it), on the Stoics' predecessors in the Socratic tradition, and in the roots of both in the ancient *Logos* (word) doctrine of Heraclitus.

Seeing all as *seeds of the Word*, they claimed that these ancient philosophers of the *Logos* tradition had prepared the way for the Gospel of Jesus. Even New Testament authors like Paul and John were themselves steeped in the Stoic tradition. Thus, the Gospel of John opens with the Heraclitean-Stoic language that ... *in the beginning was the Word (Logos), and the Word (Logos) was with God, and the Word (Logos) was God.*[18]

Stoicism's Cosmopolitan Philosophy

For the Stoic philosophy the Universe was not *Chaos,* as it was for Epicurus' doctrine of only blind force, but rather *Cosmos,* meaning an intelligible and divinely inspired rational order. Further, the Stoics saw the order of the Universe as revealing the Divine Mind, in which they saw the human mind participating like a Divine spark. For this reason, the Stoics saw the order of nature as our teacher, and so they became the founders of the Western philosophical tradition of "Natural Law," though its roots go back epistemologically to Aristotle.

---

[18] John 1:1.

In a magnanimous vision providing a foretaste of the modern doctrine of human rights, the Stoics saw all humans as equal in dignity. Grounded in this broadly humanistic vision, they then claimed that they did not belong to one "city" (*polis* in Greek), be it Athens or Rome or wherever. Rather, they claimed, they were citizens of the entire *Cosmos*, and hence were "cosmopolitan" (from joining *Cosmos* with *polis*).

So too, in a manner similar to the global Stoic vision, Christianity did not remain a closed ethnic religion. Rather, it became an open universal global religion. Then, embracing the Stoics' Natural Law, classical Catholic Christian ethics early on promoted social life at all levels as a *cosmopolis* to be ordered by political authorities to the common good. [19]

John's Stoic Vision of Global Order

It is upon this early Christian appropriation the Stoic vision of human order (seen as rooted in the Cosmic order and ultimately in the Divine order) that contemporary Catholic Social Teaching and PACEM IN TERRIS within it are philosophically based. \ Thus, John XXIII's bold Stoic vision in PACEM IN TERRIS first recognizes the emerging global era as a new and exciting stage in the human journey (implicitly postmodern). It then celebrates for this new era three important *signs of the times*:

---

[19] Later, during the European high Middle Ages, Thomas Aquinas followed the Stoics by arguing that human law participates in Natural Law and Natural Law in Divine Law. Later, during the early modern Spanish *Conquista*, the Catholic philosophical-theological School of Salamanca in Spain laid the philosophical foundation for modern international law and human rights, all based on their early modern development of the cosmopolitan Stoic vision mediated through Aquinas.

- the emancipation of workers
- the emancipation of women
- the emancipation of formerly colonized peoples

Overall, John's encyclical follows a simple outline based on the Stoic vision of order. After a brief introduction on the order of the Universe, and on order among human beings (all reflecting the Divine order), John's document addresses four concentric circles of human order.

- The first is order among human beings as individuals, with emphasis on human rights.

- The second is order between individuals and public authorities, with emphasis on the common good.

- The third is order among states, again oriented to the common good, and within that to disarmament and *true* development.

- The fourth is the order of political communities within the global community, with emphasis on the new world economy and the need for a *worldwide public authority* to govern it.

The document concludes with pastoral exhortations, especially for peace. Let us turn now to the significance of John's encyclical for Catholic Social Teaching in this new global era.

John as Prophetic Founder
of Postmodern Catholic Social Teaching

Just as Leo XIII was the founder of what has been called "Modern Catholic Social Teaching," John XXIII stands as the founder of "Postmodern Catholic Social Teaching." This new stage builds on the Leonine foundation and advances it for the new global and ecological era in the human journey.

Three Historical Strategies of Catholic Social Teaching

As outlined in my book MODERN CATHOLIC SOCIAL TEACHING, the contemporary tradition of Catholic Social Teaching, which begins with the first printed papal encyclical in 1740, has evolved through three distinct strategies correlating with three distinct stages of modern Liberal Capitalism, and correlatively of modern Scientific Socialism.[20]

- **The Anti-Modern Reactive Pre-Leonine Strategy.** First, there was the Pre-Leonine Strategy (1740-1878), meaning before Leo XIII and responding to the emergence of the early phase of the Industrial Revolution (Local Capitalism), which was grounded technologically in the Factory Revolution, with modern Scientific Socialism emerging late and only as a theory (not yet having gained state power).

  In a reactionary mode, this pre-Leonine strategy tried to preserve the authoritarian and collapsing classical aristocratic European Christian Civilization against the rise of modern secular laissez-faire liberal-capitalist societies.[21]

- **The Modern Adaptive Leonine Strategy.** Second, there came the Leonine Strategy (1878-1958), founded by Leo XIII and

---

[20] On these stages, see again MODERN CATHOLIC SOCIAL TEACHING.

[21] This strategy ended with the death of Pope Pius IX in 1878, a year which also marked the end of the Papal States, namely, the large middle belt of Italy which the popes had ruled as kings.

responding to the second phase of the Industrial Revolution (National Capitalism), which was grounded technologically in the Machine Revolution (based in refinements in steel, electrification, and petro-chemicals).

This strategy, designed by Pope Leo XIII, tried – initially successfully but ultimately unsuccessfully – to support the creation of a modern bourgeois form of Western Christian Civilization, and to overcome atheistic communism. Soviet Communism did eventually fall, but a modern bourgeois form of Western Christian Civilization did not emerge.[22]

- **The Postmodern Transformative Johannine Strategy.** Third, we are now in the Johannine Strategy (1958...) founded by Blessed John XXIII and responding to the third phase of the Industrial Revolution (Global Capitalism). This new stage is grounded technologically in the Electronic Revolution, and it is ushering in the Postmodern Global Ecological Era.

John's prophetic vision for this third strategy seeks to put the Catholic Church at the humble service of a new humanistic-ecological global civilization which will be post-capitalist and post-socialist, and which is called to seek a new global order based on justice, peace, and ecology.

---

[22] The main positive social elements of this Leonine strategy were support for the regulatory state serving the common good, support for workers unions, and support for transformation of the philosophical foundations of the modern liberal- capitalist ideology by means of a revival and adaptation of the Medieval Aristotelian-Thomist philosophical synthesis.

Still Important Strategic Themes

Seeing John as the founder of a new postmodern and global stage of Catholic Social Teaching, we may now note nine still important strategic themes in his vision as found in PACEM IN TERRIS.

- **All People of Good Will.** First, this encyclical is addressed to the entire human family, in the form of *all people of good will*.

- **See-Judge-Act.** Second, the document employs the orthopraxis method of practical theology known as "See-Judge-Act," which begins with *reading the signs of the times,* and in that reading it highlights the emancipation of *workers, women, and colonized peoples.*

- **Human Rights.** Third, this is the first papal encyclical to embrace the modern tradition of *human rights*, seen in earlier Catholic social thought as linked to the modern liberal philosophy.

  But the encyclical goes beyond the philosophical foundation of modern liberal societies, and instead grounds human rights in the classical Natural Law tradition coming from the Roman Stoics and further developed by Thomas Aquinas and the late scholastics of the University of Salamanca in Spain.

- **Disarmament & Development.** Fourth, in the wake of the Cuban Missile Crisis, the encyclical challenges the nuclear arms race and calls for East-West *global nuclear disarmament,* with its "peace dividend" to be used for *true development* in what is now called the "Global South."

- **New Global Era.** Fifth, it recognizes that a new global era has emerged for the human family, initially in the form of a *new* *global economy.* In response, it calls for a *worldwide public authority,* commensurate in scale with the global economy, and capable of directing the global economy to the common good of all.

- **United Nations.** Sixth, it highlights the *United Nations* and its specialized agencies as the beginning of such an authority, and it praises the United Nations UNIVERSAL DECLARATION OF HUMAN RIGHTS as important step.

- **New Global Civilization.** Seventh, it implicitly argues that *modern ideologies* carry deep philosophical errors, and so it calls for a *new global civilization* founded on the *true* vision of human order at all levels for the common good.

- **Dialogue and Cooperation.** Eighth, while the document rejects modern materialist ideologies, it does not reject human persons who hold those ideologies. Rather, it urges *dialogue and cooperation* with all people of good will.

  In that regard, PACEM IN TERRIS distinguishes between ideological *errors* which must be rejected and good-willed *human persons* who may hold errors but should be approached in love, dialogue, and cooperation – thus ending the Catholic ban on dialogue and cooperation with socialists.

- **Agroecology.** Ninth, as in John's earlier 1961 encyclical MATER ET MAGISTRA, this 1963 encyclical proposes (without explicitly using the term) a vision of *agroecology,* in which the human family would not be increasingly crowded into megacities, but instead would be able to find *true* rural development.

Pacem in Terris'
Continuing Prophetic Significance

It should be obvious that John's strategic philosophical vision remains even more urgent for us today, especially as we face global nuclear proliferation, the explosion of a global underclass of unemployed and underemployed youth, and a global ecological crisis which major scientists now call the *Holocene Extinction* (constituting the sixth great extinction of life on Planet Earth).[23]

Yet, in the early moments of this new Postmodern Global Ecological Era, the human family is being dragged into a catastrophic ecological breakdown, which is the equivalent of nuclear war in slow motion. At the same time, the human family faces intensifying economic, political, cultural, and spiritual crises— causing the late modern form of many human institutions to become dysfunctional, and in some cases even pathological.

These profound cultural crises mark on one side the climax and breakdown of the 500-year long wave of the modern Western colonization of the peoples and ecosystem of the Earth Community, and on the other side the birth of the still emerging and not yet fully defined Postmodern Global Ecological Era.

Meanwhile, however, the shape of a new global civilization, prophesied by John, has not yet been clarified. But, as he implicitly argued in this encyclical, the ancient Stoic cosmopolitan vision of

---

[23] This Holocene Extinction follows the last great extinction of life on planet Earth approximately sixty-five million years ago, which destroyed the non-avian dinosaurs. See distinguished Harvard biologist Edward O. Wilson's THE FUTURE OF LIFE (Vintage, 2003).

order for the common good, reflecting the natural order of the *Cosmos*, remains a valuable philosophical resource for that clarification. In addition, an important institutional resource, also endorsed by John for implementing a new global form of the Stoic vision, is the United Nations.

In conclusion, the prophetic vision of Blessed John XXIII, as found within PACEM IN TERRIS, stands as an inspiring message of hope for the entire human family in the emerging Postmodern Global Ecological Era. It behooves us, therefore, to study carefully the rich wisdom of this prophetic document, which has become even more important today.

BOOKS ON CATHOLIC SOCIAL TEACHING
FROM PACEM IN TERRIS PRESS

*The following books on Catholic Social Teaching may be ordered through the
Pacem in Terris Global Leadership Ecumenical Initiative's website:*

http://paceminterris.net/Books.html

THE VISION OF JOHN XXIII
*Prophetic Founder of Catholic Social Teaching
for the Postmodern Global Era*
Joe Holland, forthcoming in 2013

PACEM IN TERRIS
Its Continuing Relevance for the Twenty-First Century
Francis Dubois & Josef Klee, Editors, 2013

PACEM IN TERRIS
*Summary & Commentary for the 50th Anniversary of the
Famous Encyclical Letter of Pope John XXIII on World Peace*
Joe Holland, 2012

100 YEARS OF CATHOLIC SOCIAL TEACHING
DEFENDING WORKERS & THEIR UNIONS
Summaries & Commentaries for Five Landmark Papal Encyclicals
Joe Holland, 2012

THE "POISONED SPRING" OF ECONOMIC LIBERTARIANISM
*Menger, Mises, Hayek, Rothbard:
A Critique from Catholic Social Teaching of the 'Austrian School' of Economics*
Angus Sibley, 2011

BEYOND THE DEATH PENALTY
The Development in Catholic Social Teaching
D. Michael McCarron & Joe Holland, 2007

29832518R00064

Made in the USA
Lexington, KY
08 February 2014